Telling Your Story

A Guide to Writing Your Memoir Stories

Marva K. Blackmore

Library and Archives Canada Publication Data

Blackmore, Marva K. 1947 –

Telling Your Story: A Guide to Writing Your Memoir Stories

ISBN 978-0-9937449-3-8

1. Memoir Writing 2. Storytelling 3. Memoir
4. Blackmore, Marva K. I. Title

First printing: November 2016

Weaver of Words Publishers
1056 Mallard Place
Qualicum Beach, British Columbia
www.wordweaver.info
word.weaver@shaw.ca

Printed and bound in Canada
Cover Design: www.blackmorestudios.ca

Dedication

To David, with all my love

∞ ∞ ∞

Table of Contents

Chapter 1

Before You Start

*The cave you fear to enter
holds the treasure you seek.*
Joseph Campbell

Why Do You Want to Write Your Stories?

You are probably very motivated to write your stories; after all, you picked up this book, didn't you? Let's get started down the right road.

Let me introduce myself. My name is Marva K. Blackmore, and I conduct workshops on "Memoir Writing Using Storytelling Techniques." I have developed, used, and taught these techniques over several years. In that time I have learned several things about the people who come to these workshops intending to write their memoirs and family stories.

First of all, many of the workshop participants simply derive great pleasure from telling their stories. They enjoy the unfolding of the tale and find the connection with the past energizing and rewarding.

Some people come with a series of troubling memories that they wish to soothe and eventually resolve. They write their stories from deep inside themselves. These stories are often not easy to write, but once they start writing, they are motivated to continue because writing these stories seems to bring them peace and comfort. In the end, they can choose whether or not to share their stories. Sometimes, just the journey is enough!

Others are motivated to tell their stories using reasons such as "I ought to do it," or "My children want me to do it," or "It's a good thing to do." People motivated by "I ought to" and "It's good to" do not, in my experience, complete their memoir stories. If that is your only current motivation, think a little deeper. There might be another motivation driving you to write your stories that will lead you to greater success.

Finally, the most successful memoir writers are the ones who start from their own needs and believe in their stories. They believe in their stories enough to commit themselves to writing them down—for themselves, for their family, and possibly, for the world.

So, before you begin, stop for a moment. Think about why you are writing your memoir stories. Who are you really writing for? Who is your audience? Now is the time to be honest with yourself. You want this to be a rewarding experience from the start of the process to the end.

First Things First:
Your Memoir Writing Mission Statement

What motivates you to write your memoirs? Make a list. Are there enough reasons in this list to keep you writing?

Now place the items from your list in a mission statement which begins with:

"*I am dedicated to writing my memoirs because...*"

This mission statement now lists the benefits you see in taking on this memoir project—for both yourself and for others.

Mission statements can change as the project progresses and you become more aware of possibilities. Review your mission statement periodically. Change it as your project progresses so that it includes your newest motivations and possibilities.

Mission statements help to remind us where we are coming from and point us in the direction that we are going. If you don't check your map/mission statement from time-to-time, you may become lost and flounder without a sense of purpose.

Mission statements, if you choose to share them with others, may also help you to explain what you are doing—especially to friends and family who have decided that you may be slightly daft for becoming an author at this stage of your life.

More often than not, those who doubt you are just jealous because they would like to do the exact same thing, but can't get their act together. You, however, are well on your way to success. And, you have a mission statement to prove it!

Chapter 2

Are You Ready to Start?

*The secret of getting
ahead is getting started.*
Mark Twain

Tools of the Trade

Start with the writing skills you have now. Don't wait until you have taken writing course after writing course.

If you wait until you know everything you need to know about writing—well, let's be honest—you will never get anything written or finished. And, if your writing skills aren't the best, don't worry about it now. Just write using your own words and in your own manner.

Grammar, spelling, and punctuation don't matter at this stage. It's the thought that counts, and it's your job to get those thoughts written on paper. Who better to do that than you?

If you can say it or think it, then you can write it. I also promise you that the more you write your thoughts down, the easier it will become. I am not saying it is always easy, but I am saying it will become easier as you gain confidence in yourself and in your writing abilities.

When the time comes, seek out and hire an editor. We will talk more about the different types of editors and their respective roles later in this book. Their job is not to change the essence of what you write, but rather to help you with formatting and the mechanical aspects of writing. Your job is to tell your own story.

First drafts are not always the best, so don't expect that of yourself. Any great writer will tell you that. You are going to be rewriting your story at least once, and some sections will probably be rewritten several times.

You will continue to massage your story until something inside of you says, "This is how I want to tell my story." And then, once you are certain it is the best it can be, it will be time to seek out an editor.

The important thing is to turn off the editor in your own mind when you write your first draft and just write the words as they want to come out of your head.

Also, be aware that everyone around you thinks he or she is a critic and an editor. Be strong and faithful to yourself and your mission statement. Nod politely as advice is heaped upon you from others, but do not drown in their good intentions.

During the first-draft stage, say, ***"At this stage, it is important for me to get my initial thoughts down without worrying about form and format. That will all come later. It is how all the great writers do it. I am just following in their footsteps."***

Then turn and walk quietly away. Do not get into a debate with your friends and family. You have your mission statement and your thoughts and you are secure in the knowledge that you are doing the right thing. You also have my book to back you up.

Now go in front of a mirror and practice that phrase ***"At this stage, it is important for me to get my initial thoughts down without worrying about form and format. That will all come later. It is how all the great writers do it. I am just following in their footsteps."***

Once you are comfortable in front of the mirror, you will be ready to face the onslaught of the well-intentioned. Be strong and true to yourself and your mission. You can do it if you try.

Tools to Assist You

There are some very basic tools that you need to begin the process of getting ready to write. These tools will help you to stay organized and to write efficiently.

- *__A three-ring loose-leaf binder__* This type of notebook allows you to add or delete from your collections of printed stories at any time. Seeing your stories accumulate will be very encouraging. Make sure that you date each of your stories. How you organize your binder is up to you. You can organize it chronologically (date order) or by subject matter.

- *__Manila file folders__* These are useful for keeping discarded stories, story fragments, and ideas to use later. Or perhaps, you might want to refer to previously written stories when you are rewriting. Folders are always handy for organizing interview notes, photocopies of articles, letters, etc. Just remember to label them and keep them in some sort of order. A filing system is only as good as your ability to retrieve the information from it. If you can't find the information, then you might as well save yourself the time and frustration and just file it in the recycle bin.

- *__A computer__* Some people like to write finished stories by hand or even on a typewriter (for those of you who lived before the time of computers—a time when correcting tape and white-out were brilliant innovations. Remember what these devices looked like?)

Forget using a typewriter if you can. Typewriters discourage you from editing and enhancing your work. Typewriters kill the creative writing process as we know it in today's world. A first draft becomes an only draft, stifling your ability to improve upon that first draft.

Choosing the computer route need not be intimidating. Keep it simple. A basic computer is all you need—one with a word processor application and access to the internet to do research and receive e-mail. Anything more than a basic machine is up to you. Ask yourself, "Do you need (or will you use) any other features or all the bells and whistles offered by more expensive computers?"

Not using a computer is a terrible waste of your time and energy. It is possible to not use a computer, but it is really hard slogging. Most individuals will use "difficulty" as an excuse to never finish their memoirs. They will become frustrated when they find themselves typing the same story over and over again.

Of course, the main advantage for using a computer is making corrections; making changes is greatly simplified and, when the time comes, it will facilitate your working with an editor.

It is so much easier (and less costly) when you can exchange computer files via e-mail instead of stacks of paper. Computer print-outs are also much easier to read than handwritten documents. You can even change the font size to accommodate your eyesight and current mood.

If you lack the computer skills, you need to write your stories, basic instruction is readily available either at a local college, seniors center, family place, or

community center. Look for an adult education class that will make you comfortable with this important tool.

In the meantime, while you are strengthening your computer skills, you can write your thoughts down on paper and file the pages carefully in your manila folders in anticipation of entering those thoughts into the computer at a later date.

Note that it doesn't take long to learn basic text entry skills and often a weekend course/workshop at your local library is all you need to get started. In fact, computers are available at most local libraries these days, and the library would be a good place to start if you don't currently own or have access to a computer.

Libraries are also usually full of helpful people. If you don't get the answer to a question or don't understand an answer, just ask another person. Don't lose patience. Just keep asking questions.

The Memory List

The next tool is one you create yourself. This will become the backbone of your memoir stories: **The Memory List**.

The memory list is simply a list of ideas, thoughts, topics, concepts, feelings, words, or phrases that will help you to focus on those stories that are memoir-worthy to you.

People attend my workshops and often tell me, "I want to write my stories, but I have forgotten so many details. The memories seem so far away." Many of these people purchase books of lists or go to the internet seeking lists of "memory triggers." If you really want those lists, I can give you thousands of memory triggers. However, in my humble opinion, they are largely useless and do not generate the stories you are looking to write because they are not tailored to you.

Lists of words/ideas generated by others do not a memoir make, because they are not your words or your ideas. These have to come from within you. Once you start to remember, the floodgates will open. One word leads to another and one idea begets another. The secret is getting started; beginning with that first word and that first idea. It is from that starting place that the memories flow.

Having said that, I am offering you a tool that helps make the experience of writing your stories successful. That tool is **The Memory List**. No other tool opens the process of memoir writing as quickly and as easily as the thoughtful compiling of **The Memory List**.

It's simple and, as a first step, it is crucial to your success.

How to Create Your Memory List

This is a step-by-step process that is quickly and easily started and once started, happens faster than you realize.

First, the process is internal.

- Don't force a structure on it. It does not need to be chronological—you do not need to start at the beginning.
- It does not have to be thematic—you do not need to create separate lists relating to home, upbringing, work, family, friendships, etc.
- Do not strive for cause-and-effect relationships ("because this happened, that followed") unless the memories happen that way on their own.

Second, do not censor your memories.

- Don't ask yourself, "Is the story important enough to include in my memoir?"
- Don't say, "I really don't want to tell that story." If you do, that means you are censoring your Memory List.
- If you censor your list, you may be omitting something that will later be critical to the success of your memoir. You don't know what will be important while you are in the process of remembering.
- Let yourself go wherever your memories take you.
- A Memory List includes LARGE and SMALL, IMPORTANT and TRIVIAL items. Any one item in itself may not make a complete story. However, when combined with another item or

two, a powerful story may emerge. Do not discount any memory that shows itself to you.

This list can grow to many, many pages or be as short as a few entries. It can also take you two or three weeks or even months to compile. Treat it as an ongoing project. Every time you look at the list new thoughts will come to you. Add those thoughts to your list. Your list does NOT have to be complete to start writing your stories.

I recommend that you keep a small notebook on you at all times (in your purse or in your pocket). These memories will now surface when you least expect them—while standing in line to buy your groceries or sitting on a bench by the library. You can take out your notebook and jot them down and transfer them to your list when you get home. It is all a matter of doing—not just thinking about doing it.

Note these memories as just a few words or even a single word. You are not writing a complete story, anecdote, or even a vignette. Write just enough to jog your memory later. Use words like "red tricycle" or "house on Carlisle."

Whenever you sit down to write, you will never experience writer's block again. With an extensive list of memories to pick from, you will always have a list of "triggers" that are specific to you and you alone.

You will, no doubt, continue to add to this list as you continue to write your stories. With each story you write, additional memories will surface. Add them to the list so that they are recorded for future use.

Keep this list in your three-ring binder. You can also store it on your computer. However, there is something satisfying about opening your binder, thumbing through your list, having your eye fall on a particular memory, and then deciding to write that story. You might also want to make a note beside that memory about the date on which you started to write a story.

Making Sense of a "Total Memory List"

You are now going to make a smaller list based on your longer or **Total Memory List**. This list will be about the relationships and events which, had they not occurred, your life would have taken a different turn, and you would have been a different person from the one you are today. Anytime you made a decision or had to make a choice could be a potential memory trigger and should/could be added to your list.

If life taught us anything, it taught us that we have a limited amount of energy and time. We may, in fact, run out of both before all our stories are written. You need to identify your most important stories. You need to determine the stories that are about the main relationships and events in your life.

Are these the stories you want to write? If they are, then you should probably write them first. This "**Prime Memory List**" will then contain the memories that will serve as the backbone of your memoir-writing project. The other stories become peripheral stories that will be written as time and energy permit.

The "Prime Memory List,"

Your **Prime Memory List** should contain **TEN** items and no more. Fewer are fine. What types of items should be on the Prime Memory List? Only big items. For example, items like:

- A major illness or death in the family
- The arrival of a sibling
- A significant fire, flood, car accident
- A formative relationship with another person
- A failure or success at school
- Marriage/relationships
- Children/family life
- Career choices/changes
- Religious and spiritual quests

By limiting yourself to only TEN items, you are forced to evaluate and select the most significant material to start writing about now. Usually items on your **Prime Memory List** are items that involve some sort of choice or life event that is truly a "fork in the road" for you.

You may find as you review your **Total Memory List** that several items that seemed to be separate and independent are actually related to an item on your **Prime Memory List** and these items might cluster together to create one larger story.

Some Added Tools

Many people who attend my workshops find it very useful to use visual aids when writing their memoir stories.

Some people really like drawing **maps of the neighborhoods** where they lived, even being able to add details such as the names of people who lived in various houses on the block. They told me it helped them to bring back a great number of forgotten memories:

> *I remember that we used to play hide-and-go-seek until it got so dark our mothers finally had to call us in.*

> *I remembered about John Smith. I had forgotten all about him. He was only four or five when he got really sick. My mom said he went to heaven. But it was about the time of the great flu epidemic, so I think he really must have died from the flu.*

The mapmakers also liked to draw pictures of the home or homes where they lived—both as children and as adults. Again, memories came flooding back as they placed the furniture in its proper location.

Don't forget those **family photographs** that may be languishing in your storage area. Although it is a great deal of work to sort through them, sometimes just an occasional leafing through the boxes of photos (especially if you don't want to take the time right now to sort and organize everything) may again yield a long-forgotten memory. You may even be able to use the photos in your memoir.

I had that personal experience with my brothers at a family reunion. Leafing through a pile of photos, brought up a story about our great-grandparents. I had part of the story and my sister-in-law had the other part. Between the two of us, we were able to piece together the entire story for family—and it was a story that would have died with us if that picture had not been in that pile of photos.

Finally, sometimes putting your own life in the context of world events is also helpful. At the back of the book in Appendix III is a very ***short list of world events from 1900 to the present.*** When telling your stories, it is sometimes helpful to your reader if you can not only give the year the event happened, but also put it into perspective with what else was happening in the world at that time. Or sometimes, just glancing at a list of world events will also jog your memories. "Where were you when the Berlin Wall came down?"

An Exercise to Jog Your Memory

Try the following little exercise to get started. It's a technique that is often used to jog the memory of individuals who are trying to regain lost memories.

- Pick a topic of interest.
- Write that topic down.
- Now write down the first word that you associate with that topic.

- Now write down the first thing that you associate with that word.
- Continue down this track until you have 7 to 11 words written.

Work quickly: don't give yourself too much time to think about the association that you come up with. Your response needs to be visceral, from your gut, from inside you. You can make sense out of the list when you are done. If you take more than a second or two to come up with any one association, then you are over-thinking the task.

Be free and trust yourself. There are no right or wrong answers, only associations and your mind knows best so don't fight it.

Here is an example of a list of associations.

Start: Son

1. Car
2. First
3. Hudson Hornet
4. Fast
5. Traffic ticket
6. Dating
7. Steamy windows
8. Being stuck in the woods
9. Pregnancy
10. Marriage
11. Laughter

I think that you could almost write this person's memoir for them from this short list. Think how easy it is going to be to write your own memoirs from your own lists.

If you are not used to giving yourself permission to express your own thoughts, then you may need to repeat this exercise many times over a period of time, say once a day for five days.

Remember there are no right or wrong answers, just associations: your associations. Review these lists. Are they not telling a story? Are they not telling <u>your</u> story? All you need to do now is write the story that the words are telling you.

The Writing Schedule

How much time and energy are you willing to give to your writing? The more honest you are answering this question, the more pleasure you will derive from your writing. Also, you will derive more satisfaction preserving your stories.

The first step is to set a ***realistic writing goal*** for yourself. You are probably familiar with the saying, "Under-promise and Over-deliver." If you follow the same philosophy with your writing and set realistic writing goals, you will find yourself less frustrated and less disappointed later.

Creating a Writing Schedule

Here it is—step-by-step.

- Create a weekly and monthly writing schedule.

- Be specific about dates, days, and hours.

- Write this schedule on your calendar.

- Advise members of your household and be willing to negotiate or to offer something in exchange for their cooperation and support.

- Pin the schedule to your household bulletin board or refrigerator.

That's the easy part.

First of all, it is important that you practice writing. Everyone, and I mean everyone, gets better with practice— skating, painting, singing, and yes, writing.

You need to practice at least 15 minutes per day. You can even write while you are having that first cup of coffee in the morning. Buy yourself a journal and write in that. You will notice that your writing becomes better, easier, and more fluid the more you write.

No need to be critical of your writing at this stage; that will come later when it is time to focus your writing on a given topic. For now, just write. Make yourself a short memory/association list and just start writing. What are the words in your list telling you? Write the story.

No need to rip out pages or use "whiteout" to cover changes. Just scratch out something if you want to and keep on writing. Give yourself permission to make mistakes and say silly things or serious things or anything at all. This is for you. This is practice. This is a learning tool that will help give you confidence that you can do this thing called writing.

You know you can do it because you are doing it now. And, if you don't "do," well then it is time to review your Mission Statement.

What was it that you wanted to do?

What Happens When I Sit Down to Write?

The First 60-90 Days

- Your schedule is done. You are ready to start writing. You go to your computer. You have set aside 30 minutes to write today. *You turn on your computer.*
- *You start your word processing program.*
- *You DO NOT start your web browser.*
- *You DO NOT check your e-mail.*
- *These 30 minutes are for writing only.*
- *You also send your "editor in your head" away. You will give him or her a call when required—BUT NOT TODAY.*
- *You place your hands upon the keyboard.*
- *You are ready to type.*

By the way, if you can't type, it is never too late to learn. There are several free "learn to type" programs available on the internet. Or, you can choose to use the hunt-and-peck method of typing favored by my husband. If neither of these methods appeals to you, you can now use the more sophisticated speech-to-text programs. You can purchase products such as Dragon Naturally Speaking or search for a free program on the internet. But what you may not do is look for any of these resources during your writing time.

Continuing on with your writing time, here is what you do next:

- Think of some event that is unusually vivid in your memory. Any event will do. It could have happened yesterday or 60 years ago—any event as long as you remember it vividly. Do a quick list of associations if you find that technique helpful. (This should take less than a minute!)

- Recall the memory and write it. Describe what happened and how you felt about it. It doesn't need to be long—one page, two pages, five pages. But the episode should be complete in itself. One story with a beginning, middle, and an end.

- When you finish, date it, print it, and put it in a manila folder. Get on with your life. Don't edit it. Don't re-read it.

- The next day, do it again. The memory doesn't need to be related to the previous day's memory. Take whatever memory comes knocking. Make a list of associations if you like. Remember that you want a beginning, a middle, and an end to your story. Do not let your stories trail off into "nothingness." Give each story an end. It is important to have a sense of completion for each story that you write.

- Forget that you are embarking on a larger project—the memoir. I promise you that it will all come together at a proper time.
- When you are finished with your story, date it, print it, and put it in the folder.
- Do that every day—preferably around the same time of day.
- You are now exercising new muscles—all part of the practice—memory muscles, writing muscles, organizing muscles. These are your writing muscles!
- Your subconscious is also working while you are sleeping—poking around in those memories you stirred up.

You are going to keep doing this for two or three months. The time will pass quickly. Be patient and keep writing. Work on your memory list and use the association list technique to help provide a blueprint. Always ask yourself, "What are the words telling me?" Write the stories in your own words.

Don't be impatient to start that memoir you had in mind. You are in the process of getting there. After all, what is a memoir but a collection of discrete stories?

After two or three months take all of your entries from the folder and spread them out on the floor. Here is what you will discover:

- Your first entries are stiff and awkwardly written.
- The entries you write later are more relaxed and sound more like you.
- The entries you wrote in the first month may never be used by you but you needed to write them to get to the entries you wrote later which you may be able to use. It was like stretching before you exercise.
- Gradually you are finding your "style." All that means is the person you want to sound like on paper, which is the person you really are, is finally coming out of you. Writing is like talking to someone else on paper. You simply needed to learn to talk like yourself when you write.

Certain themes and patterns may start to emerge in your stories. Your own material will begin to tell you, "That's a good direction," or "That's a funny story," or "That's fascinating." It will also tell you what is not interesting or what is boring or what is off limits given your current circumstances. While everything deserves to be written, not everything is meant to be shared.

You will also begin to see if stories don't fit into certain patterns. If you are telling stories about growing up in the west, then the story about sailing the ocean doesn't likely fit. You may find that you actually have more than one memoir.

"I'm confused," you say. "I thought everyone only had one memoir."

No, that's one autobiography.

- An autobiography is a story **of a life**. The author attempts to capture all the elements of importance in his or her entire life.
- A memoir is a story **from a life**. It doesn't replicate a whole life; just a piece of it. So maybe you will need to write about your different life pieces separately.

Time to Review Your Writing Schedule

After you have been doing your initial writing for two or three months for 30 minutes a day, you are now getting excited. It's time to really get serious about writing and polishing your stories. But now is not the time to sit at the computer for eight hours a day non-stop for a day or two and then find yourself exhausted and burnt out.

You need to take a serious look at your writing schedule. You need to set aside writing time and ensure that it is time that you protect for your writing.

You also need to make sure that you are being realistic about how much you can or want to write in a day or at a single sitting. You also want to ask yourself if you want to give yourself weekends off and holiday time.

- Don't think in terms of "I'll write as much as I can." Be honest with yourself.
- Base your writing schedule on a specific amount of time or a page quota (or a word quota).
- Decide how much time you have each week to devote to your writing. If you have a day that is already committed with activities that you are reluctant to give up, then schedule them in (maybe this is one of your "non-writing" days).
- A realistic schedule will maximize your chances for success. However, remember that both laxity and rigidity will work against you. Commit your schedule to paper and write the schedule on your calendar. This schedule needs to become part of what defines you for the next short while.

If you need to "borrow" time from your writing schedule on any one day, remind yourself to "pay it back" before you allow yourself to "borrow" again. Make the change "official" by making the change(s) on your calendar. You want/need to commit to the change.

Being lax with the "credit" system will set you up for failure. You will become overwhelmed. How can you possibly "pay back" 30 hours? In the end, you may find that you are no longer doing any writing at all.

Rigidity will also work against you. If the words are flowing, continue writing even if you have met your page or time goal for the day. Stopping in the middle of your creative process doesn't make sense—quota or no quota. And while I think of it, if you are stopping mid-story, never end with a period! If you stop mid-sentence, you will find it easier to pick up where you left off the next time you start writing. This will force you to reread that incomplete sentence (sometimes you may need to reread that partial sentence many times) and this in turn will get you back on track.

This simple technique may sound silly, but if it works, why not take advantage of it? Unless, of course, you aspire to be one of those long-suffering authors that throw up all sorts of self-imposed obstacles that will assure you a life of trials and tribulations.

My advice to you is to avoid the misery, enjoy the writing process and be happy. Developing good writing habits early on will go a long way to ensuring your success.

In the "credit" system, give yourself a bonus if you put in some "overtime." This means that you can later take time off from writing if the mechanics of living interfere with your writing schedule. And, no, you don't get time-and-a-half for overtime.

- Pursue your writing step by step, day by day.
- Make decisions that contribute to your success.
- Remember, the writing you are doing is not only fun, but it is also important to you.

And Now You Write

From here you start to write your stories in earnest. The next chapters will look at some of the tools you could use to enhance your writing and storytelling.

These are methods that storytellers began using even before stories were written. Many of these were developed when storytelling was mainly an oral tradition, but these tools are still useful in today's world because the elements of a good story have not changed.

These are also tools that successful writers have been sharing to make storytelling better and more readable—however, you needn't stray from the truth.

As a memoir writer, you don't need to make-up details, characters, and events to please the readers or to keep their interest. You are not writing pulp fiction (that is another type of writing). The truth is all you need.

But before we continue—a word of caution about one modern tool available to you.

The Internet

The time-waster. How many of you have spent hours and hours on the internet looking for family background, specific dates, information, and doing fact verification?

I am here to tell you that when you are first recalling your stories and writing them down is <u>NOT</u> the time to surf the internet. It is a major ***procrastination*** tool and it will take away from your writing. I know it is easier to read information from the internet than to write your own memoirs. However, now is not the time for internet research. You already have the memories. Now is the time for writing.

If you need to check a fact after you have written an idea or a story or a vignette down on paper, then so be it. However, get what you already know down on paper before you go searching for more material. In memoir writing, fact checking takes place after you have written something down, not before you write.

Turn off your access to the internet if it distracts from your writing. Turn off your e-mail, your Facebook, and anything else that pulls you away from writing during your designated writing time. Writing time is for writing!

While taking the time to write your daily story, or fragment of a story, or snippet; you are no longer going to be searching the internet looking through reams and reams of pages on memoir helpers, how-tos, memory triggers or birthdates. You don't need them at this point. Now, you need to just write.

When it comes time to finalize your stories that will be the time to check dates and facts—not when you are writing down the stories as you remember them during your designated writing time.

Chapter 3

Start Writing

Don't worry about failures, worry about the
chances you miss when you don't even try.
Jack Canfield

Did you take the time to think about and to create your Mission Statement? If you did, you now have a clearer idea why it is important for you to write your memoir stories.

But in the back of your mind, there is the little question that keeps popping up. Is my writing good enough?

My answer to you is, "Don't worry about whether your writing is good enough." As you write, be comfortable letting your first drafts be "first drafts": rough, incomplete, and contradictory. If you think in terms of "good enough," you will find yourself in a trap that will prevent you from writing or writing frequently.

Unfortunately, you have an inner censor who lives in your head. This censor judges your every action, and it is the censor who asks, "Is the writing good enough?"

It is your censor that holds you back, instils fear, and tells you that you may look silly. Your inner censor expects you to write elegant prose on your first attempt.

Tell your inner censor to relax! It doesn't work that way. You are not competing for the Nobel Prize in Literature, the Pulitzer Prize, the Governor General's Award, or the Booker Prize.

Be aware there are really two censors. There is the critical censor who says your writing is not "good enough." That is the censor we have just been discussing.

There is also the censor that says, "You should never write about that. Your family (mother, father, sister, brother, daughter, etc.) would never approve." No one, and I mean no one, will see what you write until you show it to them.

So write away. Later you can determine what to do with your work, but for the moment, you write for your eyes only. The time for sharing will come later.

However, in the interests of being honest with yourself, you should write whatever you remember to the best of your own ability. Whether or not you choose to make it public or reveal it will be up to you. But to not acknowledge a memory or event is being dishonest with yourself. We will deal with the issue of "truth" in memoir writing in Chapter 6.

Let's talk about some of the more common fears you will likely face as you write your stories. If one of these describes something you fear, then it may be time for you to face it head on.

1. **Fear of Inadequacy.** There is something very permanent about putting your words on paper. If you only tell your stories orally to people who will listen to you, then the stories are not permanent. You can choose to never tell the story again if people don't like

it. Or, you can make some minor alterations that will make the story even better. But as soon as you put it down on paper, there is something permanent about the story that makes it very intimidating.

2. **Fear of Criticism.** It hurts to be criticized. Even "constructive" criticism hurts. What if the family doesn't like what you have written? What if the public doesn't like it if you choose to send your memoirs out into the world? You control that. You can write your memoir stories. You can read them out loud to yourself or to a few chosen friends or to no one. You are completely in control of what happens to the stories you write. You will also have the opportunity to revise, rewrite, and edit anything you have written before it leaves the privacy of your desk. Never forget, you control who sees your work.

3. **Fear of Success.** Some people never let themselves succeed at something because they are unsure and uncertain what the next steps will be after a success. In the words of my departed mother-in-law, "Wait to worry."

A lot can happen between now and then and you will drive yourself crazy if you over-think life after a success. Besides, success is all relative to your expectations, and your expectations are clearly stated in your Mission Statement. Leave that Mission

Statement out where you can refer to it so you can keep yourself grounded.

If your memoir is a run-away bestseller, then you can worry about what to do about it at that time; i.e., writing your next one. If that happens, you may be motivated to continue writing the rest of the stories you wish to write. You didn't get where you are today by being unsuccessful. Embrace the possibilities, but stick with your Mission Statement. You can always change the Mission Statement to meet your current needs and expectations.

4. **Fear of Making Mistakes.** Yes, you will make mistakes. We all make mistakes. That is why first drafts are called rough drafts. Some people even call them "zero" drafts—pretending they don't even exist.

Don't let perfectionism stand in the way of getting started. You can plan forever. You can make mind maps, flowcharts, and outlines. You can fill note cards with ideas. You can also collect interesting ideas and log them into your computer, but until you sit down and start that first story, fear of making mistakes will be one of the driving forces against you and that is a force you must overcome.

What is the worst thing that can happen? If you make a mistake, you will rewrite it. No big deal—you are in control. Right?

5. **Fear of Commitment.** We are all busy. Yes, you are going to have to make a commitment of time and energy to this task. That is why I asked you to sit down and create a realistic writing schedule. I didn't tell you to give up your life, but to make sure that you set aside a realistic amount of time in your life for your writing. And then I asked you to stick to that writing schedule. If you found that circumstances meant that one day you had to deviate from your plan, then you must quickly make up for lost time. Set up a time credit balance system for yourself. This is time you owe to yourself. If it means giving up something else in your life for the time being, then sit down and realistically decide what needs to be put on hold.

    Being productive is never an accident and the first step to being productive is to make a commitment.

6. **Fear of Having Nothing to Say.** If you have taken the time to create your **Total Memory List** and your **Prime Memory List,** I am convinced that you will always have something to write about. Just simply go to your list (which will actually continue to grow as you continue to write) and review it. You will always find a

new story on that list. If anything, you may have the opposite problem of having too much to say.

Have you ever noticed that those people who tell you they have nothing to say often end up talking the most? Why is that? Well, it usually starts by someone saying, "Sure you do," and then they ask that person a question. The answer leads to another question and another answer and, before you know it, the person is suffering from verbal diarrhea.

You have a story to tell, so you definitely have something to say. You just need to start writing it.

7. **Fear of Being Too Old.** You are never too old to sit down and write. The saying, "You can't teach an old dog new tricks," does not apply here because learning new tricks is always linked to motivation and not age. You can't teach teenagers anything if they aren't interested in learning. The same applies to our aging population.

Regardless of your age, if you have made a commitment to yourself, then the writing will come. You just have to give yourself permission to write. You can't reach the goal line if you don't start.

You can choose to write for 15 minutes, 30 minutes, or one hour per day. Choose a time that is comfortable and doable for you. On the other hand, if you find yourself becoming consumed with your writing, it is probably more important you take the time to schedule breaks so you are not sitting for long periods of time.

In conclusion, my best advice to you is to face your concerns and fears. If you find yourself spending a great deal of time organizing your writing files, planning your work, and cleaning your office, you are probably afraid of something.

If you are finding more excuses for not writing your memoirs than reasons for writing them, then you have a problem that needs to be addressed. It is sometimes best to just stop and name whatever it is you fear. What is keeping you from your writing? Naming your fear is the first step in facing it. Once you name it, fear is truly easier to face and like the monster under the bed, once you confront it, it will disappear.

How Do I Start?

You have now been writing for a few minutes every day for the last 60 to 90 days. You have been crafting vignettes, scenes, dialogues, and small stories. This helped you to practice the craft of writing, to create your memory lists. You are becoming comfortable transferring your thoughts onto the written page. I had you layout your writings on the floor in the order you had written them. You could see then how your writing had improved and changed over that period.

I also suggested you might have seen certain themes emerge. You might also have noted scenes and vignettes that logically went together.

Now is the time to put those writings in order by theme or by story. For instance, "This is the first part of this story, and this is what happened as a result, a couple of years later."

Or maybe several of the stories are related to a difficult time in your childhood or your children's early years or an illness you had to deal with. You can now gather these similar themes together and begin to think about the transitions or linking stories between the individual pieces you have already written.

As you continue to write and generate more and more pages of text, you must decide if one story is better than another. Is a story too short or too long? Does it have a logical beginning, middle, and end? Is there a dramatic arc in the story? Does something actually happen or is it just a character study? Is the main character changed in any way as a result of what took place in the story?

This is where all rewriting and editorial work begins. This review process has its proper place in writing, but you can't rewrite something that has not yet been written.

These rough drafts are going to be the building blocks on which your memoir is going to be built. Identifying relationships, weaknesses, strengths, and gaps in your writing so far will now help direct future writing.

Write Your "Up Front" Stories First

New writers tend to gravitate toward stories they have already told. These are the stories they share at cocktail parties, around campfires, and at family reunions. Why do they write them first? These stories are the easiest to write. They are familiar stories they are comfortable with and they generally know how the listeners will react to them.

If these are the stories you are writing, the words just seem to roll from your fingers. They appear magically on the paper or the computer screen.

"Why did I think writing was so hard?" you ask. "I should have started doing this years ago."

The reality is you have been rehearsing these stories for years. Every time you told the story, you watched the people listening. If they appeared bored, you may have sped up the story. The next time you told the story, you may have eliminated the part of the story or the back story where people became inattentive or where your significant other kicked you under the table. You may have chosen to enhance the parts where they were very interested or even laughed. If the story was too long, you shortened it. If you found that a certain order of revealing details built suspense, you altered that order. You may have actually been working on the story for years.

This is how professional storytellers create and hone their stories. The first time a professional storyteller tells a story, it is not perfect. The "rule-of-thumb" amongst the storytellers is a story must be told at least fifteen times before it is ready to tell on the professional stage. And, the story is rarely exactly the same each time it is told. It is okay to make changes because it is your story.

You may have already done your "rewriting" orally for many years. Most of the preparation was done ages ago, and the stories are already highly polished. Is it any wonder you can write these stories with relative ease? How often have friends and family told you that you should write "that one" down?

You may find the stories you write later more difficult but only because they are less polished to start with. You will only have spent a few hours, rather than years, preparing them. As you practice writing your stories though, you will write better stories earlier and earlier in your writing process. Do not get discouraged that some stories take longer to edit than others. Generally speaking, older stories take less time to edit and new stories take more time.

Let's look at two important issues before we continue on: "Point of View" and "Voice."

Point of View

When I talk about point of view, I am NOT referring to your political viewpoint or your ideas about a particular subject. I am talking about "point of view" in writing. It refers to the perspective from which a story is told, and it comes in three varieties: "First Person," "Second Person," and "Third Person." Some writers find it easier to think of the three varieties as "I,"

"You," and "He or She." However you do it, you need to be aware of these three different points of view and decide which one you are going to use for a given memoir story.

Using an inappropriate point of view when telling a story will only confuse the reader and muddle the story in your own mind which, in turn, will make it difficult to write.

To choose a point of view, you need to understand the differences amongst the three. Your use of personal pronouns (i.e., I, you, or he/she) will define the point of view of the story.

First-Person Point of View

This is the point of view to use when a person/character is narrating the story. For example, when writing in the first person you use the words/pronouns "I-me-my-myself-mine." The story is being told as if the narrator is telling his or her own story.

These pronouns are called "personal pronouns" because they define who the narrator is to the story. When an author uses the pronouns "I, me, mine, my, or myself" in the writing, the author is writing in "The First Person."

Using the first-person point of view means the reader gets to hear the narrator's thoughts and see the world through the eyes of that person.

However, the narrator cannot have complete knowledge of everything. The narrator can only know what the narrator knows at the time the story takes place. The narrator will not know what another character is thinking although the narrator will know what another character does if the narrator witnessed the events (or was told by someone else). You know what you are thinking but you can only conjecture what someone else is thinking.

Most memoir writers choose the first-person point of view since these are their stories as they remember them.

Here is an example of what speaking in the first person might sound like if you are trying to express a moment of grief. It is also written in the present tense (as if it were happening right now).

> *Jack is dead but I feel like I am still seeing him everywhere I turn. I shiver and loneliness washes over me in waves. Will my grief never end? He haunts me night and day. Yet I still hear him calling me from beyond the grave.*

"Memoir First Person"

Let's look at the first-person point of view from a little different angle. When we talk about the "who" of who is writing your memoirs, then you need to carefully consider who is writing the story; i.e., from whose point of view is the story is being written?

Is it the "adult you" sitting here today recalling stories from your childhood? Or are you telling the story as if it is the "child you" telling the story as if you are still that age? Or is it the "teenage you" telling a story, for example, about being bullied?

Those points of view may change how the story is told. A child telling a story will not have the years of reflection the adult has, but a story told by a child often has more immediacy and is more compelling than the story by the adult in reflection. A child's story is more "black and white" and does not usually contain "the grey" that is derived from adult philosophic introspection.

As an example, consider the following passage from Jeannette Walls' memoir, *The Glass Castle*. Here is the back story to help you put this example in context.

In the first line of the memoir Ms Walls, as an adult, spots her mother dumpster diving in New York City, and ignores her. The next scene is of little Jeannette, age three, cooking hot dogs for herself. This is life as normal in her odd household. She accidentally sets herself on fire and then we meet her father, the unforgettable Rex Walls, when he comes to the hospital to visit her. Although she has been badly burned, he thinks his little girl should have been taken to the witch doctor that cured her older sister's scorpion sting. He threatens to beat the doctor for saying that bandages are required.

Through Jeannette's words we see him (and hear him, smell him, touch him, and very nearly taste him) as she writes in the first person as a young child:

> *A few days later, when I had been at the hospital for about six weeks, Dad appeared alone in the doorway of my room. He told me we were going to check out, Rex Walls-style.*
>
> *"Are you sure this is okay?" I asked.*
>
> *"You just trust your old man," Dad said.*
>
> *He unhooked my right arm from the sling over my head. As he held me close, I breathed his*

familiar smell of Vitalis, whiskey, and cigarette smoke. It reminded me of home.

Dad hurried down the hall with me in his arms. A nurse yelled for us to stop, but Dad broke into a run. He pushed open an emergency-exit door and sprinted down the stairs and out to the street. Our car, a beat-up Plymouth we called the Blue Goose, was parked around the corner, the engine idling. Mom was up front, Lori and Brian in the back with Juju. Dad slid me across the seat next to Mom and took the wheel.

"You don't have to worry anymore, baby," Dad said. "You're safe now."

We see the man in action, but we see him from the little girl's point of view. She doesn't judge her old man—he's a hero, her knight in shining armor. Later, Ms Walls will write from an adult point of view: "In my mind, Dad was perfect, although he did have what Mom called a bit of a drinking situation."

Second-Person Point of View

Authors rarely use the second-person point of view which uses "you," "your," "yours," "yourself," and "yourselves." Authors rarely speak directly to the reader. If an author chooses to use the second person, it has the effect of drawing the reader into the story and almost makes the reader a participant in the action.

When you write letters or e-mails you most likely use the second person; e.g.,

Charlie, don't forget your lunch. You also need to ask the doctor about your hives, so be sure and

> *make an appointment for next week if you know*
> *what's good for you.*

Advertisers sometimes like to write in the second person to get you involved.

"*Have it your way*," says Burger King, and Nike tells you to "*Just do it.*"

Which I must say, "It sounds like good advice." Let's do this!

Third-Person Point of View

An outsider looking at the action is called the third-person point of view. The reader watches the story unfold as an outsider and the author is omniscient (all-knowing). That means the author knows what every character is thinking, saying, and doing at all times. When you are using pronouns like "he, she, they or it," you are usually writing in the third person.

For a writer of memoir stories, this is a very impersonal way to write, and the reader will feel that your stories do not ring true. It will feel like you are trying to put distance between yourself and the stories you are writing.

If the stories are about you, then you really should write them in the first person. If you are writing a family history that is a different genre. You are still writing stories, but you may or may not be the main character in the stories you are telling.

In other words, when you write in the third person, you are writing "their" story. For example, Jane Austen, author of *Pride and Prejudice*, wrote this from the character, Jane Bennet's, perspective about Mr. Bingley:

> *He is just what a young man ought to be," said*
> *she, "sensible, good humoured, lively; and I*
> *never saw such happy manners! – so much ease,*
> *with such perfect good breeding!*

Jane Austen wants to present to you Ms Bennet's point of view so she wrote this passage in the third person. The "said she" indicates the third person. You, the reader know to take what is being said as Ms Bennet's voice and not the personal recollection of the writer.

If you want your memoir to be personal, use the first-person point of view.

Voice: Active and Passive

Active Voice

I will start with the active voice because it is simpler. In an active voice sentence the subject is doing the action. In other words, the subject underlines performs the stated action.

A straightforward example: "Bob hit the ball." Bob is the subject, and he is doing the action. He hit the ball, the object of the sentence. Bob is performing the stated action. Bob is actively doing the action.

A second example is "I heard it on the radio." "I" is the subject, the one who is doing the action. "I" is hearing "it," the object of the sentence.

The active voice is usually clearer and more concise. Most writers will use an active voice wherever possible.

Passive Voice

In the passive voice, the target of the action gets promoted. It becomes the subject of the sentence. Or, in other words, the subject is <u>being acted upon</u> by the verb.

Instead of saying, "Bob hit the ball," I would say, "The ball was hit by Bob." The subject of the sentence becomes "the ball" but it really isn't doing anything. Rather, it is the recipient of Bob's big wallop. In the passive voice, the focus of the sentence has changed from "Bob" to "the ball."

If you wanted to make the second sentence passive, you would say, "It was heard by me on the radio." Not very forceful. Passive sentences aren't incorrect. They just aren't the best way to phrase your thoughts. Sometimes the passive voice is vague.

The passive voice can also be wordy, so you can tighten your writing if you replace passive sentences with active sentences.

When you put sentences in the passive voice, it can be easy to leave out the person doing the action and this leads to confusion on the part of the reader. For example, "The ball was hit," is passive. The problem is you don't know who hit the ball.

The use of the passive voice can also create awkward sentences. Your writing may seem flat and uninteresting. Political writers and governments have been known to use the passive voice when they do not wish to assign blame and use sentences such as

"Bombs were dropped," or "Mistakes were made." They never specify "who done the deed!"

In memoir writing, encouraging conjecture by the reader is rarely a good approach unless you are trying to obfuscate the facts and create confusion.

Avoiding the use of the passive voice also helps avoid **dangling modifiers**. A "dangling modifier" is a word or phrase that modifies (or describes) a word not clearly stated in the sentence. For example, "To save time, the memoir was written on a computer." (Who was saving time? The memoir?) In the active voice, the sentence would read, "To save time, Ellen wrote her memoir on a computer."

Chapter 4

Let's Talk About Plot

All the words I use in my stories can be found in the dictionary—it's just a matter of arranging them into the right sentences.
W. Somerset Maugham

Beginnings, Middles, and Ends

I will bet you have heard this one a lot: stories have beginnings, middles, and ends. Do you ever wonder what this really means and how do you make sure your story has a beginning, a middle, and an end?

Let's look at the basics. We will get into more details shortly.

Successful stories usually have a <u>beginning</u> you can recognize: *"My mother was still having trouble with her eyesight even after the baby was born."*

This is then followed by a <u>middle</u> that tells what happened in the story: *"After the diagnosis of myasthenia gravis, she was sent to a hospital about 80 miles away. Her mother, my grandmother came to stay with my brother, our newborn brother, and me. Dad traveled to see her every weekend."*

And finally, an <u>end</u> that reveals how the story concludes: *"When the baby was only two months old, we got a call in the middle of the night. She had passed away. Our lives now entered a whole new era none of us had envisioned. My Father had lost his wife, and we had lost our mother."*

In fact, in this case, the end of the story might also be considered the beginning of the next story.

Stories Have Action

Successful stories have action. A story without action or conflict or a dilemma is usually just a series of facts or a listing of events.

Travelogues often become just a series of dates, times and places. Where's the story in that?

Readers want to know what happened in your travels and how you overcame adversity. The real story is about you. Think of yourself as the protagonist. What happened in your travels that brought about change through an active decision on your part? Did you come to a new understanding about yourself, the world, or your place in it as a result of your experience?

The time, place, and setting should be relevant to what you did there. Sure, those travel facts are interesting and add spice to the story, but they alone do not make a good story. In the case of a memoir, actions tell your tale far better than a list of facts. Use the facts to support your actions, and you will create a better memoir.

A lovely piece of writing may only be an essay (your thoughts on a subject) or a character piece (a description of a person, both a physical description and his or her actions or behaviors) or, in some cases, nothing. It could also just be a well-written boring piece of writing. Don't get me wrong, essays and character pieces have a place in literature, but not in your memoir. Your memoir needs to centered around what you did, not just the places you visited along the way.

Most interesting memoir stories are centered around a plot. The central hinge of any story plot is a crisis. However, don't be too narrow when you define "crisis." Cleaning up spilled milk can be a crisis worthy of a story.

A crisis is any event which takes a part of our lives with which we are comfortable and turns it upside down. After the crisis, we must adjust to a world that is shaped differently than it was before.

What are some examples of a crisis?

- Winning a lottery
- Getting married
- Having a baby
- Retiring

- Buying a new house
- A death in the family
- An accident
- A new job or a new boss
- Being a cancer survivor
- Spilled milk and a thousand other things that brought change to your world.

When the crisis happens, we watch the main character (you) go through the throes of the critical event. Usually there is a tension brought about by the circumstances leading up to the crisis and in turn, a decision or resolution of some kind is or was made. After making that decision, your life was altered and change happened.

> *...after spending two hours cleaning the kitchen and removing the spilled milk from the heating ducts, from under the fridge and stove, and fending off the somewhat aggressive cat visiting from the absentee neighbor, all the while comforting the hysterical child in the high chair while being held in a life or death grip of my three-year-old toddler, I came to the conclusion that my mother-in-law's advice stating that naps were for sissies did not merit consideration and this set the stage for a debate on child rearing that lasted well into my adulthood. The afternoon nap with the children curled up in my arms and the cat asleep at my feet became a family institution and confirmed that I could make meaningful independent decisions on my own. I was in control.*

The main character gets help, acquires new learning, and does something that never could have been acquired or done without struggling through this particular critical event. As a result, life is never the same.

Take a moment and think back to some of your best stories that you told over the years—the stories the family appreciated the most. Did they contain any or all of these elements? Think about the stories that fell short. Were they missing some or all of these elements? What changes might you make to those stories to better describe what you went through and better depict how the resulting outcomes affected you and those around you?

Over 99% of the stories you encounter will fall into this traditional story structure. The other 1%? They are usually experimental pieces that are less successful unless they are written by incredibly talented authors who understand story structure.

You might have heard a sports coach or an English teacher say, *"You have to know the rules before you can break them."* That is absolutely true in writing stories as well. It is best not to try a shortcut until you know the established route. So for now, think **first-person, active voice, and a story with action and outcomes.**

Seeing Your Story as a Pyramid (Freytag's Pyramid)

Gustav Freytag invented this tool to better understand Greek drama and the plays of Shakespeare. The pyramid identifies the five main dramatic parts of a story. After you master it, you can start seeing it in sitcoms, movies, books, plays, and in your own work.

Although Freytag's Pyramid is a useful way to see your story's narrative or dramatic arc, it's not enough to come up with the five parts and say that you are done. The pyramid is NOT a plug and chug, paint by numbers, formula that guarantees success. It is, however, a useful way to get started and/or review stories with an eye to making them better. Here it is: Freytag's Pyramid.

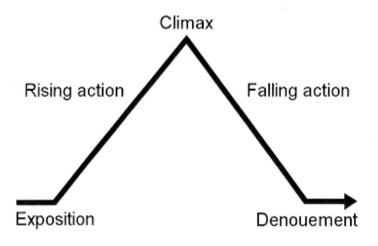

Starting the Story:
Exposition and Inciting Action

Two things happen at the start of your story: Exposition and inciting action.

Exposition is the information given at or near the beginning of the story to show the normal life of the main character or at least the state of the person.

The inciting action is the change that happens that launches the story. Incite means "to start up" or "to provoke." In other words, the incite leads to "action(s) rising."

Here is an example from the Harry Potter stories:

Young Harry has a lousy life with the Durleys who dislike magic and treat him horribly. (Exposition)

Harry receives his invite to Hogwarts, and he enters the world of wizardry. (Inciting Action)

In this example, take out the inciting action and you have a regular, normal life that is not worth an entire book or story.

Increasing the Emotion:
Rising Action

This is the long, gradual heightening of emotion, suspense, and tension. Typically, this is the largest segment of your story—it takes a while to set everything up right for the climax. Rising action may represent up to 50, 60, or even 70% of your entire story. However, each part of your story needs to bring you (the protagonist) and the reader closer to the climax.

The main character is striving to meet his or her goal, but finds obstacles in the way. In other words, the main character has a goal, and the rising action is about the challenges that keep that goal from being reached.

With a memoir, the rising action is probably those parts of your past where you say, "If only I knew then what I know now!" But you didn't know how to circumvent those problems, people, and obstacles and that kept you from success. That led to drama, and that drama leads to reader entertainment.

When someone reads your memoir they expect to learn something about you (the author). The reader expects this and yearns for this understanding. So give them what they seek but build the suspense along the way.

"Will you do something or won't you?"—that is the question in the readers mind.

Reaching the Emotional Peak: The Climax

The emotional high point, the turning point; this is the climax. This is the opportunity for the greatest change in both the story and the main character. Because the tension and intensity are so high at a climax, these parts of the story are necessarily short but poignant.

Having a character controlling her or his own life versus just reacting to events that happen along the way is far more rewarding, though in a memoir, you have what you have. You need to stick to the reality of what happened to you.

How you tell and organize your memoir will make all the difference between a boring memoir and an interesting one. This approach may also help you decide which stories you write.

Starting to Resolve:
Falling Action

If rising action is about heightening the tension and emotions in the story, then falling action is the exact opposite. The loose ends are being tied up. The outcome of the climax may suggest one ending, but there's still hope for another. The major conflict of the story is finally being resolved. What path will be taken? The resulting consequences (and unintended consequences) may need some further refinement before a successful resolution is obtained.

Wrapping up Everything:
Resolution

The resolution of a story is where things finally get figured out—at least enough to satisfy your reader. Conflicts are finally settled which allow for the release of all the built-up tension from the story. This is typically a direct result from what happened in the climax. Also, this needs to be a logical conclusion based on the information as you have presented it. A resolution that comes out of nowhere is going fall flat with your readers.

If the story is a "comedy," then the main character is better off than when he or she was at the start of the story. If the story is a "tragedy," the main character is worse off than he or she was at the beginning of the story.

In essence, the resolution of a story purges the readers of any emotional worries they had over the happenings of the story.

It means that all the complexities of the story are managed and done away with. It can be a happy occasion, but it can also be marked by hope, sadness, regret, or damage.

Eyeing the Importance of Plot

Plot is a series of causes and effects. Plot is the main story arc that occurs in a memoir.

Story is what happens. Plot is the point-by-point happenings of the story. These points form a line when connected: the plot line. If your readers can't see the connection between each of these points, if the line becomes broken, they won't be happy and they will stop reading your stories. They expect a logic to govern the story. It is your job to provide that logic.

A memoir has the added complication of encompassing what really happened. Sometimes life arranges the scenes or events in a very inconvenient way. Life doesn't always follow an orderly "Freytag Pyramid" plot line. But you can still strive to find elements of the conventional plot in your own memoir story as it happened in real life.

A complex story is not always the best story. Don't add complexity that takes away from the story or destroys your plot line or story arc. When *inciting action, rising action, climax, falling action,* and *resolution* can be readily identified, you would do well to take advantage of the opportunity. Don't mess with a good thing.

Red Riding Hood—Pyramid Exercise

Let's look at Little Red Riding Hood—a folk tale that has been around for hundreds of years, and let's use Freytag's Pyramid to analyze the story. Many folk tales, fairy tales, and children's stories follow the pyramid. Readers appreciate the structure and clarity the pyramid delivers—and it delivers it in spades.

Try to remember as much of the story as you can. Then write down the main plot points. Finally, using Freytag's Pyramid, place those plot points on the pyramid. Then see how you did below.

- Once upon a time, there was a dear little girl, Red, who was loved by everyone. *(Exposition)*
- Grandma was sick and Mother sent Red off with a basket of goodies. She warned Red to stay on the path. *(Inciting Action)*
- Red went through the dark woods to Grandma's house. *(Rising Action)*
- She met the Big Bad Wolf. *(More Rising Action)*
- He convinced her to take a different route so she could pick flowers. He hurried ahead to Grandma's house. *(More Rising Action)*

- He ate Grandma and dressed up as her. *(More Rising Action)*

- Red arrived and did not realize it was the Wolf at first. *(More Rising Action)*

- Red noticed Wolf's big ears, eyes, hands, and teeth. *(More Rising Action)*

- Wolf ate Red. *(Climax)*

- A woodsman came by and heard Wolf snoring. As soon as he figured out what happened, he cut open Wolf and freed Red and Grandma. He took the wolf skin home. Red and Grandma ate the treats. *(Falling Action)*

- Red learned never to leave the path again. *(Resolution)* *What a great story!*

The Journey of the Hero

Here is another way to look at your story plots. It is similar to Freytag's Pyramid, but it has some variations that you might find useful.

Many people say that all the plots in the world are all based on one basic plot—the journey of the hero. This is a straight narrative plot form and, if you do any reading at all, you most certainly have encountered it.

Joseph Campbell in his book, *The Hero with a Thousand Faces*, described the essential core of the great folk stories as a journey of transformation. He believes it is the fundamental story type, central to our understanding of what life is all about.

From Odysseus returning home from the Trojan Wars to Star Wars, the journey of the hero is repeated in every age and culture. You begin as one thing and end up as another. You start in one place and find yourself compelled to take a journey—either by choice, by chance, or by necessity. In the process you discover your true nature, your strengths, your weaknesses, and your capacity to change.

You have an adventure.

The heroic journey contains five steps:

- The Invitation
- The Exchange
- The Challenge(s)
- The Triumph
- The Return

The Invitation

In this part the hero or heroine gets a call to adventure and decides to leave home to do great deeds or win a prize.

The journey may be the child who leaves home to make his or her way in the world. It may be just a journey down the block to discover a new part of the neighborhood or it may be a journey to a far and distant land. It may be a man who must answer a question or seek a solution to a problem. It may be a person who needs to heal a wound and who sets out on a journey to accomplish this task.

What is the action that sets this story in motion? Is it based on opportunity or discontent? Is it accidental or deliberate? The invitation sets the scene or plot.

The Exchange

As the hero travels along, he or she meets someone who will ask for help to perform a task. The journey will now move from an external to an internal focus.

When crafting a personal story using the "journey of the hero" model, ask yourself:

- "Whom did you meet along the way?"
- "Who were your mentors and helpers?"
- "Did someone ask you to do a small task that was the beginning of an important relationship?"
- "Who offered you advice or gave you tools for success on your journey?"
- "What did you receive?"
- "Did that person know what he or she gave you?"

A Series of Challenges

The hero or heroine then faces a number of challenges that must be overcome, each one more difficult than the last or at least testing a different aspect of his or her character. How many, you ask? Culturally, the number of challenges is a "core number" of a cultural tradition. What does this mean?

If you look at the cultural tradition of European and American folk stories, three is the core number—three wishes, three bears, three pigs, etc. With three as the core number, there are usually three challenges.

Think about the challenges you faced on your journey. Can you pinpoint three challenges that are symbolic of your journey?

- Which ones raised the stakes?
- What was at risk?
- What would be an appropriate progression from external to internal challenges?

Sometimes when you are writing your memoir stories, you have to take your reality and massage it or rework the story (not change it or add in elements that never existed), to create that magical "core" number of three. Two major challenges and a minor challenge still make three challenges, right?

Take the time to think about the challenges and how they fit into your journey as you write your story.

The Triumph

All this leads to the deciding event in which the hero or heroine accomplishes what he or she set out to do—finding the treasure, locating your best friend's house further down the block than you were ever permitted to go, getting your tree house built, winning the race, answering the question, slaying the dragon, or winning the hand of the beloved—by using his or her own inner resources.

When you are crafting your own heroic journey, what is the moment of triumph? What is your definition of success? Is it a sudden and decisive event? Or is a quieter moment of understanding? Is the victory sweet or bittersweet?

The Return

Having accomplished the task and having been transformed, the hero or heroine returns to where he or she started. This act of completion is necessary. For the sake of balance, the journey should end where it began in relationship to the community or culture left behind.

The return is the completion of a cycle. You cannot afford to skip or discount this portion of the journey. It provides an emotional balance and a sense of closure to the journey.

Where Does My Story Start?

When you start your story, your goal is to ensure that the reader is gripped by what you have to tell them. You need to make the opening scene compelling enough for the reader to want to continue reading what you wrote. You must engage the interest of the reader.

Start by Introducing a Character

Characterization is very important and later I devote a whole section on how to create "three-dimensional" characters and how to make them come alive through your writing. If you plan to use your opening paragraph to introduce a character, remember that you are still trying to write a compelling opening.

The person must be relevant to the story and not simply be there to cause a sense of drama. Your readers are smart. They don't read just for the shock value; they are looking for real information that will fuel their desire to read.

Think about a dramatic moment that affects one of your characters in your story and make the opening relevant. In memoir writing the character that you are probably introducing is yourself!

William Zinsser begins his memoir, *Writing About Your Life*, with the following lines.

> *Every so often I find on my answering machine in mid-Manhattan, a brief cry for help. "What should be used to stop water stains coming through the ceiling?" the voice asks, or "Is it O.K. to use primer-sealer 1-2-3 for peeling paint in the bathroom?" I don't know anything about water stains and peeling paint; I'm a writer. The callers are trying to reach William Zinsser & Company, my father's shellac business. The company was in New York so long—well over a century—that some old customers think it's still there, and when they call directory assistance, the number they're given is mine. I'm the only William Zinsser still doing business in New York; the firm moved away in 1975 and was later sold out of the family.*

With that beginning character sketch, you have an initial glimpse into Zinsser's location, the time, his family, and what he does. Now on to the story. And, by the way, it is one of the books I highly recommend as an example of an excellent memoir plus good information for your own memoir writing.

Start with Conflict

Conflict always works well in the opening paragraphs. The readers know immediately what to expect and what type of story lies ahead if they carry on reading. It doesn't always have to be dramatic (someone drowning or hurling themselves to their death), but conflict between characters can also be gripping.

However you introduce the conflict, it must again be relevant to the story that will unfold, rather than just be used to create sensationalism.

Maybe Your Starting Point is not at the Beginning

As you write your story and then get ready to rewrite your story, you may still be looking for the best place to start your story. Sometimes the best place to start, from the reader's perspective, is not at the beginning, but at some moment of decisiveness.

Whether you are looking at Freytag's Pyramid or The Hero's Journey as a model for your story, there is always a point where things come together or things fall apart for the character(s) (possibly, you) in your story.

If you want to "hook" your reader, start writing close to the final crisis or "climax" and then start at the beginning and proceed toward the ending.

The reader will want resolution so at some point your story will need to catch up to your opening statement. This is a favorite opening strategy of authors who write "thrillers," but it works for memoir writers too!

As an example, you could start with a sentence like,

I didn't know my life would be completely changed that day...

or

I always dreamed of being a test pilot, but I never dreamt that I would find myself hurtling towards earth out of control and scared out of my wits. Visions of my family passed in front of my eyes and time stood still as I struggled to reach the ejection handle. It was then that I felt the blackness of unconsciousness invade my mind.

Whether you choose Freytag's Pyramid or The Hero's Journey as a model for your memoir, the start of your story is going to set the tone of the story and needs to capture the reader's interest in a hurry. First impressions are lasting and it is difficult to capture (or recapture) a readers interest once it is lost. With a little forethought and planning, that will never happen to you—"right?"

Chapter 5

Successful Stories

are More Than a Plot

*Memoir isn't the summary
of a life, it's a window into
a life, very much like a photograph
in its selective composition. It may
look like a casual and even random
calling up of bygone events. It's
not; it's a deliberate construction.*
William Zinsser

The Characters in Your Life

It would seem that writing about the different "characters" in your memoir would be one of the easiest things to write. After all, you don't have to create them. They already exist. But in fact, putting the characters into your stories is much more difficult than it seems at first glance. Your job is not only to describe them, but also to make them come to life on the page and to integrate them into your story in a manner that supports your story.

The first thing that makes a reader read a book is the characters within a plot. If you are standing at the airport, or in the bookstore, or browsing books on-line, you are hoping to find a book where you will like the characters. You want to find a book with interesting people in it. If you pick up two books with a similar plot, you will always choose the one which depicts the characters in a manner that captures your interest.

If it is a book, you can physically pick up and thumb through, you might read the back, browse a few pages, maybe read the first page or two, and see if you are intrigued. If you are "on-line," you can look at the front cover, and read the back cover, the description, and sometimes a few pages. If the characters interest you, you are more likely to purchase the book than not.

Humanize Your Characters

Successful stories have characters that are recognizably human. However, human beings are complicated; characters are simple. Human beings have tens of thousands of traits. Characters in a book have less than a hundred, with one or two traits that predominate their essence. You get to select the main descriptors. It is best to pick wisely.

Don't let your loved ones become "stick figures" or caricatures in your stories. Make them real to us and make us care about them.

If you are writing about them, you must have some sort of feelings about them—warm or otherwise. If your story is about a person in your life, make the reader care about what happens to that person. If readers don't care about the character they are reading about, they will simply stop reading entirely or skip to another part of the story they find more interesting. No matter how great the plot, if the character is not worth caring about, the reader ceases to have any investment in continuing to read. It is as simple as that.

Even if you are writing about people you don't particularly like, don't just show their faults. Give the reader a fuller picture of the person. Show some of the positive qualities of the character as well as the negative.

If you just dwell on the negative, the reader will not believe that your characters are real and, again, will dismiss not only what you say about the people, but also whatever it is you want your story to convey.

> *Mary had the disposition of a wounded monkey and verbally abused all who came within range, but she loved her animals. Her furry menagerie could do no wrong, it was people she lashed out at and unfortunately, I was 'people'.*

Write about People, Not Just Events

People want to read your stories especially if they include people that you met in your life. Your story is defined by the people around you. Thus, you need to not only describe the characters in your story that you encounter, you also need to describe yourself in relation to those people. If you do not have sufficient character building, your stories will seem weak, hollow, and plodding. Showing the characteristics of the people in your story and your relationship with them will also help define the story you are writing.

Many people writing their memoir stories focus on the events and forget about the people in the stories. The characters or people, however, are as critical to your story as the events. Remember—events never happen in isolation from people. In short, people need events and events need people.

It is the CHARACTERS who want something. They drive your story forward. They want, they desire, they yearn, and they covet. From their desires and needs, your story will unfold. Your characters will ring true if you include a sense of motivation—money, power, love, or status. What makes them tick?

Describing Characters

All of your characters need to be described and all characters are inherently different. But, the difference between a good and bad description is a fine line. Too little description and your reader won't get the correct picture of your character. Too much description and you will bore your reader to tears. Often writers will give a head-to-toe description of a character the minute he or she steps into the scene. This has the effect of stopping the action. So be careful.

Instead, you need to look for ways to let the information about the character come out gradually in the context of your story; possibly by the way the character acts in the story as much as by a long-winded detailed description.

For example, as opposed to saying your uncle was an exceptionally tall man, make a statement that he had to duck under the door jamb every time he entered the room. Your reader will understand that he was very tall. In fact they will understand his height far better in relation to a door jamb than if you simply stated that his height was 206 centimetres (approximately 6 feet 9 inches). I can see him ducking his head below the jamb. What do you see if I say, "My uncle was 206 centimetres tall?"

Further, consider using similes or metaphors. A simile is where one thing is compared to another. The words "like" or "as" are used in a simile; e.g., *David cried like a baby,* or *Beth was busy as a bee.* On the other hand, a metaphor contains an implied comparison between two things; for example, *The parking lot was a zoo,* or *Ralph was so hungry he could have eaten a horse.*

Here are some other examples.

- (Straight Text) *Bob was 6 foot 6 inches tall and weighed 260 pounds.* (You do get a picture of Bob as a big man, but you can do better.)

- (Simile) *Bob was built like a football linebacker.* (Now I have a better picture of what he might really look like.)

- (Metaphor) Bob is scary big. If you push him until he loses his temper, he could rip the New York phone book in half. (Now I know more about what Bob acts like as well as being big.)

Characters Don't Have to be Famous

The time you met John Lennon in the elevator and he signed your autograph book may have been an interesting anecdote—but was it life changing? If it was, then there is a story. If not, well then it is just name-dropping and doesn't move your story forward.

That reminds me, did I ever tell you about the time my husband met Muhammad Ali in an elevator in Chicago? My husband just stood there mute and unassuming.

Note that my telling you this anecdote was a waste of your time and did not move this book forward. (Other than it serves as an example of worthless information being worthless.) This was not a life altering experience for anyone (especially for Muhammad Ali, my husband or me and now, not you.)

It is more important you portray the characters that influenced your life and your decisions in an interesting fashion. You need to make me care about them so that I want to know about them and what happened to them and you as the writer of the memoir story. The people who made a difference in your life are where my interests lie.

Show, Don't Just Tell

You may have also heard people use the phrase, "Show, don't tell," and you have probably nodded your head in agreement; but, secretly you have wondered what that really means.

The marvellous thing about memoir stories is that we already know what our characters have done. We are simply telling the story, organizing the events, and writing down the drama. The events really happened.

Even better, we know exactly (as best as we can remember) how they happened.

- You remember how your mom held her mouth when she was annoyed or when she really didn't believe a word you were saying.
- You remember when your dad was going to explode with anger over your last shenanigan.
- And you knew that look on Great Uncle Sam's face when he was pulling your leg.
- You specifically remember when the principal walked down the corridor with his hands behind his back surveying the teens at their lockers, making sure they were the appropriate distance apart; you can see the stride in his walk, and when he stopped to separate an errant couple, you can see him take a breath before he speaks.

You know these things because you were there, and you observed them.

Now you have to tell your reader what you observed. The trick is not to just describe your observation, but to describe those events with "feelings."

Use your words to let them see the same picture you are seeing in your mind's eye. Make your readers feel like they are right there with you—observing the scene, seeing the principal take that breath before he steps forward to scold the couple for being too familiar in the hallway.

This is telling:

I was very nervous as I waited to go on stage.

This is showing:

My hand trembled as I lifted the bottle of water to my lips. My stomach felt like it was full of butterflies, and I was certain I was about to lose my voice. The master of ceremonies announced my name and, afraid of falling flat on my face, I carefully stepped forward onto the stage.

As you can see, showing takes you much deeper into the moment. Telling is bland. You don't actually experience what the person is going through. You don't get a real sense of the fear and the nervousness.

Let's try another example.

Telling:

> *The grizzly bear stood in front me on the path.*

Showing:

> *The grizzly bear looked enormous as he stood*
> *up and raised his forepaws high over my head.*
> *He stood directly in my path, and he looked*
> *like it was his intention to stop me from going*
> *anywhere.*

In the first example, I am told some information. In the second example, I actually begin to feel a little bit fearful. What is the bear going to do? What is the writer going to do? This is a problem that needs a solution—and some quick thinking.

Recreate the Event

Instead of merely reporting an event, do your very best to recreate it with words.

Don't just announce, "I found her hiding behind the garage."

Tell your readers the whole story. Tell them exactly what happened. Perhaps it might have gone something like this:

> *I went out into the backyard to find her. I*
> *rummaged through the spirea bushes. She*
> *wasn't there. I struggled up the beech tree—*
> *climbing the six wooden blocks nailed to the*
> *trunk—until I reached the tree house. It was*
> *empty. The sun was beating down hotter than*
> *ever, and I was getting sweatier and angrier by*
> *the minute. Then, out of the corner of my eye,*
> *I glimpsed a piece of red cloth disappearing*

behind the garage. I rounded the corner and there she stood, frozen in a running stance.

Showing Tells the Truth

"Showing" not only makes your story more interesting than "telling," it also makes it more believable. By showing, you are "proving" your point – whatever that is – perhaps, your sister was the source of all your unhappiness or your best friend was the one person you could trust.

When you make generalizations and only summarize events, you are essentially telling your reader, "This is how it was because I say this is how it was." Telling means that the event was not that important. Showing says that this event was important to you and the story that you are telling.

But readers need proof. They will not take your word for it. They want to form their own opinions based on the evidence that you present. You need to show them in your story why what you are saying is true and important.

In the words of Mark Twain, "Don't say the old lady screamed, bring her on and let her scream."

Coming to Your Senses

All we have to believe is our senses:
the tools we use to perceive the world,
our touch, our memory. If they lie to
us, then nothing can be trusted.
Neil Gaiman

Successful stories are full of sensory details—utilizing all five of your senses: sight, sound, touch, taste, and smell. Readers want to experience colors, shapes, textures, smells, sounds, and flavors. This is where we finally truly begin to understand the statement "Show, don't tell."

When your stories portray a world filled with sensory detail, it makes it easier for the reader to imagine and create a mind's eye picture. It is better to refer to the "bouquet of sweet-smelling Star-gazer lilies" rather than a vague description such as "some nice flowers."

Beginning writers will veer away from concrete details, believing this makes their stories somehow more universal. But, in fact, the opposite is true. Those concrete details help the reader create pictures in their minds—and pictures are universal.

How many of us have read a book and, when it is finished, we have a vivid picture of the characters and the setting.   Later, when a movie is made from the book, we are disappointed. We say, "That is not how I pictured the main character and the farm was much, much different."

Yet, if you were to read an author's description, both the reader's picture and the movie director's image might, in fact match perfectly. What's that saying? "It's all in the mind's eye."

The key to writing "the shows" instead of "the tells" is the senses — all five of them.

> *I remember the alleyway as a dark, dank place. The acrid smell that came up to the window was of stale garbage and urine. You could almost taste the air it was so thick. The piercing yowls of the alley cats as they pawed eagerly through the garbage and the incessant yelling of the homeless man as he pawed hungrily through the same garbage made me feel so desolate.*

Now there is a picture for you. That sentence uses adverbs (words that modify or describe verbs) and adjectives (words that modify or describe nouns) to show you a picture. However, descriptive details are not just a matter of using adjectives and adverbs. Often the descriptive information is better given with a lively verb.

> *The smell of stale garbage and urine assailed my nostrils.*

Or

> *The alleyway frightened me. Its darkness and dankness overwhelmed me.*

These are revisions you will make when you do your rewrites. When you are doing your first rough draft, just write. Don't worry about fine tuning your language. Just get the story down on paper or into the computer. When you come back, that's when you will take the time to look at the "show, don't tell" aspect of your work and ensure that you are making full use of your senses.

Saying it Well

The best memoirs make use of good dialogue. However, writing dialogue is not always easy. Badly written dialogue is like drawing stick figures when you are describing your characters; i.e., there is no meat on the bones or substance to your writing.

Dialogue is used to move the plot forward and increase the conflict in the story.

If you are going to use dialogue to advance your plot, include verbal exchanges to increase story tension. Whatever is being said must expand what the readers need to know about the plot or makeup of your characters.

You can also use dialogue to show what your characters think or believe happens. For example, is it an overheard conversation at a birthday party or at church?

When teaching someone to write good dialogue, it is sometimes best explained by showing them examples of dialogue to avoid.

Stilted Dialogue happens when people sound too formal. In this exchange between a couple, they overuse each other's names, something that would never happen in a normal conversation between a normal couple. They also speak without contractions. People who have been together a long time frequently speak in shorthand or even complete each other's sentences.

> *"That was Doctor Jones on the phone, Harold.*
> *He says the biopsy he took shows that the*
> *tumor is not malignant. It is benign after all."*
>
> *"Thank you, Marjory, that is excellent news. I*
> *was not looking forward to dying so young."*
>
> *"Well, Harold, I take this as very good news,*
> *also."*
>
> *"Marjory, Michael Mitchell, our life*
> *insurance agent at Johnston & Sons, called*
> *last night. He told me that you have doubled*
> *the policy upon my life. Is that true,*
> *Marjory?"*

Try to avoid stilted dialogue unless, of course, that is the mood that you are trying to portray. The language needs to be appropriate to the context of any given part of your story. I must tell you that I am not a big fan of profanity, but if I am describing an encounter with someone whose normally uses that type of language, then that is the language I should use.

> *Donny told me that George was full of shit*
> *and if he ever saw that mother fucker again he*
> *would shove the fucker's head up his ass.*

The editor in me wants to question Donny as to whose ass was going to be violated, his or George's, but let's face it, no one challenges Donny and that is the way he talked. Can you ever see Donny saying the following?

Donny told me that George was sadly mistaken
and if he ever saw George again, then the
misunderstanding could be addressed.

If I wrote about Donny in this way, anybody who was reading my memoir and knew Donny would laugh at me and I would lose all credibility with that reader. This last passage does not ring true to Donny's character. It is usually best to keep the characters "in character."

Banter or Small Talk is a form of dialogue that does not have any escalation value. It doesn't move the plot forward and, quite frankly, does not have a place in your memoir story. All this dialogue does is take up time and is boring. Read the exchange below. Do you even care who is talking? It has been described as riding an exercise bicycle: it's no fun and you don't get anywhere.

"How are you?"

"I am fine."

"Good. How's your mother?"

"She's fine. And yours?"

"OK. How's your dad?"

"Great. And the dog?"

Are you bored yet? I can almost guarantee you that your reader is.

Information Dumping happens when the writer tries to deliver important information through dialogue. It is better to just communicate this information in exposition (explanation) or show it in a scene and let the characters speak for themselves. Here is an example of too much information or information dumping.

> *"Harold, Doctor Jones, who lives next door, phoned while you were at your office in the most expensive building in New York City, and said that the biopsy he did on Tuesday on the tumor in your right kidney has turned out to be benign."*

> *"Darling, that is great news. Come here with your svelte figure and lovely long auburn locks and give me a kiss!"*

> *"Be careful, your horn-rimmed glasses that you've worn since the skiing accident in Aspen are gouging my prominent forehead."*

Can you visualize how this dialogue could be delivered without all the information that is excess to the important bits?

Dialect or Stammers should not even be attempted. You can indicate how people talk, but a suggestion that someone speaks with a heavy Scottish brogue is enough. Do not try to replicate it in your writing. You might add an occasional "Aye" here and there or add selected unusual vocabulary that is germane to the character or to your story, but trust the reader to do the rest. Please, please, do not attempt to write in dialect. It is incredibly difficult to read. Have you ever tried to read a piece written entirely in 'Old English'? Here's a sample from Chaucer's *Canterbury Tales*.

> WHAN that Aprille with his shoures soote
> The droghte of Marche hath perced to the roote,
> And bathed every veyne in swich licour,
> Of which vertu engendred is the flour;

Whan Zephirus eek with his swete breeth
Inspired hath in every holt and heeth
The tendre croppes, and the yonge sonne
Hath in the Ram his halfe cours y-ronne,
And smale fowles maken melodye

I know, that technically this is really only "Middle English," but it is still hard to write and hard to read. Your story is being told by you. Keep yourself in character.

The same goes for trying to recreate a stammer or a stutter. Again, a suggestion is all that the reader needs to put your story into perspective.

Dialogue Tag Lines are used to tell the reader who is speaking. Occasionally, you may use a tag line to indicate VOLUME such as "whispered" or "shouted." But the general rule is *"The fewer dialogue tags you can use, the better."*

Well-written dialogue is seldom embellished by dialogue tags consisting of an adjective or an adverb.

"You are a useless, good-for-nothing, lazy slob," he said angrily.

The use of the adverb "angrily" is redundant. The description of the subject is enough to get your point across to the reader in this case. You know he was angry without having this nuance shoved down your throat. Readers find it insulting if you continually tell them how they should feel about what they read. Your words should reveal the situation without preaching at them.

However, if you wrote:

"You are a useless, good-for-nothing, lazy slob," he said, laughing.

That changes the complexion of the sentence since the adjective is contradicting the content of the sentence. In this context, language tags are useful because you are trying to get a point across that is contrary to the normal interpretation of the words you wrote. If you didn't use a tag, you would be giving the reader the wrong information or impression.

The following denotes something entirely different again from the earlier examples.

"You are a useless, good-for-nothing, lazy slob," he said lovingly.

Only use dialogue tags when they are not redundant to what you wrote.

There is nothing wrong with repeating <u>he said</u> and <u>she said</u> over and over. <u>He said</u> and <u>she said</u> provide fine rhythms and when repeated, they fall into the background of the reader's consciousness. If you get fancy with tags such as "she queried," "he exclaimed," and "she chortled," you shake the reader out of the reading rhythm that has been established.

On the other hand, the use of <u>said</u> can become tiresome when it appears repeatedly on the same page. And, when used improperly, it can also be a giveaway that you're an inexperienced writer.

"John said," does not equal "said John."

To hear how your dialogue reads, try inserting the pronoun instead of the character's name. For example:

"That's an amazing painting," John said.

"That's an amazing painting," he said.

Both of these examples make sense. But look at what happens when you write it the other way around:

"That's an amazing painting," said John.

"That's an amazing painting," said he.

If you wouldn't write "said he" then don't write "said John." Stick with placing the speaker's name before the verb unless there's an overwhelming reason not to.

It is also possible to use dialogue tags not only to simply indicate who's speaking, but also to create pauses reflected in actual speech or even to orchestrate the pace and movement of the scene.

"Come here," she said. "Right now."

"Come here right now," she said.

Placing the dialogue tag in the first example creates a pause that emphasizes the last two words and establishes their importance in the speech of the speaker.

People Don't Explain Themselves

When writing dialogue, keep in mind that people rarely explain themselves. They often reveal as much about themselves by what they don't say as they do by what they do say. Dialogue is what people say and how they say it. It is a way to show a character's actions. Sometimes what is not said by a character is as important as what is said.

Using dialogue can also help relieve what seems to be a great deal of text. You can break it up with some dialogue since it is punctuated quite differently from straight paragraph writing. I won't get into the various nuances of punctuating dialogue in this book. For now, concentrate on the actual dialogue and don't worry about the small stuff like punctuation.

If you really want to bore your readers and make your characters dull, have your characters spout messages, platitudes, clichés, explanations. Dialogue is for advancing the plot. It is NOT for delivering your messages, particular points of view, or explaining your behaviour or that of your characters. For example,

> *Tommy said, "I don't belongs here." He said it like that because he was from Newfoundland and Newfoundlanders often add an "s" on to their verbs. I am not sure exactly why that is but as Newfoundland was one of the earliest settled communities in North America and one of the most isolated, I think that this practice may be rooted in the Irish or Old Rural English manners of speech. He then ran through the door scattering the newly washed clothes behind him like windfall in a winter storm.*

You can clearly see how the explanation of Tommy's speech patterns distracts the reader from what is going on.

Don't feel compelled to explain dialogue as long as the dialogue advances the story that is enough. Here is the alternative.

Tommy said, "I don't belongs here." He then ran through the door scattering the newly washed clothes behind him like windfall in a winter storm.

Don't Forget to Show or Tell What Your Characters are Doing

Characters of action are always more compelling than those doing nothing. I am not talking about showing your character picking her nose or crossing her legs (unless it is germane to the story)—just to take a respite from the dialogue. But, if your character folds her arms to indicate a closed body position and an unwillingness to listen, then mention it.

Actions described during dialogue should reveal the intention of the character. Don't confuse your reader by inserting needless movement. If the action doesn't convey anything essential, leave it out.

Sometimes it is not only about what the character says, but it is also about what they don't say.

- How did the person act when he or she spoke?
- Was there a gesture, a small lip quiver, a smirk?
- Was there a nuance that could change the whole meaning of the dialogue that was delivered? For example, did the character wink as he delivered the fateful prediction?

Always ask yourself, "What value does the description of the action add to the story?" If you can't answer the question, leave the action out of the narrative.

Practice Writing Dialogue

When you are learning to write dialogue, people say, "Just write like you talk." However, people don't talk in a manner that is easy to write. For practice, record a conversation (get the permission of the people you are recording first) and then transcribe it word by word.

Try boiling the conversation down to its essence without losing the personality of the speakers. It is much harder than it seems; however, it is a very good exercise. It will also give you good insight into what does and does not work on the written page.

Dialogue Tips

Here are a few handy dialogue tips to tuck away. Keep them in mind and bring them out to use when you are getting ready to write dialogue in your stories.

- Don't use fancy dialogue tags.

- Good dialogue is conversation with the boring parts removed.

- All dialogue should advance the plot.

- Dialogue tags exist to tell the reader who is speaking, not how they are speaking.

- Always be consistent naming your characters. Don't use a full name one time and a nickname another. That is very confusing to the reader. You are not writing a Russian novel where characters can be called by two or three different names.

- If you do use nicknames, keep the names context specific. For example, if you introduced a nickname that your spouse called you, then only use that nickname when your spouse is talking about you or to you. Don't let other characters use that nickname as it quickly becomes confusing. The exception is when you use your nickname consistently throughout the entire memoir; i.e., "My name is Maggie McGuiness, but everyone called me 'Mags'."

- Don't use the character's names too often.

- Always read your dialogue out loud as a final reality check on what you wrote. Your ear will pickup mistakes the eye misses!

Indirect Dialogue

Indirect dialogue is speech that is introduced by the word "<u>that</u>." Quotation marks are not used around words that have been attributed to a person who spoke them. Here are two examples:

My daughter said that she never wanted to have any children. (Indirect)

My daughter said, "I never want to have any children."
(Direct)

Both sentences say the same thing, but the nuance is different. I find indirect dialogue is not as forcibly felt as compared to a direct quote. With a direct quote the reader is not in doubt as to what was said. Indirect dialogue has a feeling of hearsay. Both approaches should have a place in your writing; you just need to decide which approach is best to use in the context of your story. And, too much of either one is probably a bad thing.

Writers will use the indirect quotation if they are so unsure of the quotation that they are reluctant to attribute the specific words to the character. They will also use it to soften the impact of a piece of dialogue.

However, using the indirect quotation means you sacrifice immediacy and impact, and it is often less attractive to writers than the direct quotation. Chose the appropriate approach accordingly.

Chapter 6

Truth in Memoir

You own everything that happened to you. Tell your stories. If people wanted you to write warmly about them, they should have behaved better.
Anne LaMott

Every story has three sides — your version, the other person's version, and the absolute truth.

Although no one has perfect memory, you need to stay as close to the facts as you can remember.

A memoir is a promise to the reader that you are writing the truth as you absolutely recall it. Anything else is dishonest — both to yourself and to the reader.

There are, however, some liberties that you can take. For instance, you may take some liberties with dialogue. If you are creating direct dialogue — putting quotation marks around things that are being said by others—it can be assumed that, unless you have recordings of people saying these things or their written journals or diaries, you are making some assumptions about the actual conversation that may have taken place.

Some writers, of course, choose to use indirect dialogue which is definitely an indication to the reader that they are paraphrasing what might have been said.

However, if you deviate too much from what you actually remember, you are moving into the territory called "creative non-fiction" or "historical-based fiction" which is a whole different genre of writing. In either case, you must be very clear with the reader when you have stepped out of memoir and into another genre.

"Story-Truth" vs. "Truth-Truth"

"Truth-truth" is along the lines of a court transcript or what a historian tries to document.

"Story-truth" is less concerned with 100% accuracy of what happened and more concerned with portraying the experience accurately.

For most writers, it is the experience of the moment versus the fact. For instance, it was December 23 at 3:00 a.m. and there was a 95% chance of snow and the temperature was 32°F (0°C). Sometimes that level of detail may help create authenticity, but it might be better to write, "That December morning was cold enough to make my bones ache and my face go numb," and then get on to what really matters.

You are writing a memoir so people can get to know you and your story. Do not compromise on that. Let them get to know the real you, not some idealized, romanticized version of you.

You are not trying to recreate yourself. You might as well know now, no matter what you do, one-third of your readers are not going to like what you write. And, if you change what you write in order to please that third, it will just be a different third that doesn't like what you write.

I call this the "Rule of Thirds." It is a fool's game to try to please everyone, so just be strong and true to yourself and your story. The naysayers will fall as they will. Your job is to tell your own story; the story as you truthfully remember it. Here are some guidelines to help you write the truth in your memoirs.

• **Facts are the baseline of truth.** As the temperature on a cold day can be verified by reading a thermometer, facts can also be verified by referring to authenticating sources (people, documents, records). Sometimes issues that families often debate are really a matter of public record.

Did Dad graduate from high school in 1944 or 1945? Arguing the date is a waste of time; it can be authenticated by a visit — or a phone call — to his high school or by checking his graduation yearbook.

Did your family live at 327 Lincoln Street starting in February 1932 or 1933? The research needed to determine the true date might be as easy as going through family correspondence and finding a letter dated March 1933. Maybe your favorite aunt writes about working on getting the moving boxes unpacked?

If someone in your family seriously disagrees with you on the facts about dates or locations, do all that you can to verify your version. Be even more certain if these facts are important to the dramatic arc or conflict points in your story.

It is one thing to correctly remember something and quite another when you "build" memories through conjecture or supposition. Keep in mind that these recollected events are just memories and, if these recollections are germane to your story, it is your responsibility as the author to get those facts correct.

Believe me, having to print an addendum is not only humbling, but it may call into question other parts of your memoir. Do it right the first time and you will be a happier author.

If you can't find documentation to verify certain facts, then you must attribute your version of the truth to yourself. Using a statement such as "I believe that my grandparents moved into their Lincoln Street residence in February of 1933 because..." will help to quell any negative comments from others in your family who may disagree with you but may not be able to prove otherwise. If you don't remember something specifically, say that. Your readers won't think any of the less of you, but get the fact wrong and you will hear about it forever!

- **Learn to distinguish the difference between truth that is relevant and truth that is irrelevant.** In some matters, digging too deeply can sometimes be a waste of time. For example, do you really need to authenticate whether it was John or James who threw the rock that hit you and gave you the black eye and headaches? John says it was James; James says it was John.

In other words, after fifty years, a fog may have rolled over your family's collective memory. Beyond idle curiosity, who threw the rock may be irrelevant. More interesting may be how your family members reacted. It may be more relevant to know why the rock was thrown in the first place and what happened after.

- **Attribute to someone's opinion what cannot be authenticated.** Whenever you decide that pursuing the truth is irrelevant or impossible because the events occurred so long ago or everyone involved has now passed away, you may consider using such phrases as "My brother Mike always believed that...," or "My mother always said that..." Remember that your ultimate goal is to record your version of the truth— not someone else's.

However, if your version of the events is predicated on the beliefs of others, it may be important for your readers to know where your beliefs came from.

If someone else disagrees with your version of events, try not to get too defensive. You can always suggest that they write their own version since it is not your job to write their version of how the events happened.

Facts are facts, but when it comes to subjective interpretation, in your memoir you are in charge. Own your own story and not the version as others see it. They can write their own memoir and you can be helpful by recommending that they start by getting a copy of *Telling Your Story* by Marva K. Blackmore. You don't need to be confrontational; you just need to be helpful.

Being Respectful of Others

It is important that you be respectful of others who are included in your memoirs. If you are describing a person, the important thing is to do it with compassion. What does that mean? It means to describe the entire person. You have heard the expression, "That quote was taken out of context!" Well, a person taken out of the context of the whole person may be just as misleading.

Your mother may have been difficult to deal with when you were a teenager and her punishments may have been or seemed to be unreasonable, but you need to look at her as a whole person. She had been your mother long before you became a teenager. Was her behavior always mean or had something changed in you? What was her background? Was she raising you as she had been raised? Did things change when you became older? Just saying that you had a "mean" mother is probably selling her and yourself short.

A very good book which explores all the issues around truth in memoir is *The Truth of Memoir* by Kerry Cohen. She not only gives her own ideas, but explores the ideas of many other memoir writers who have written about how to address writing about others and about sensitive issues.

In general, you need to get your point across to the reader without being self-destructive to yourself or to others. The key to that approach is to understand not only what you went through, but what the others in your story went through as well. If you feel that you are painting someone into a corner, it is best to allow that person an avenue out to "save face"; e.g., "I am not sure what motivated John to throw that rock, but he sure came across as mean-spirited."

If you include stories about people who are still living and if you still know how to contact them, you might consider taking the following steps.

• Notify them in advance of publishing the memoir stories and detail the parts which might make them or you uncomfortable. Treat these interactions as fact-finding missions or research. Take notes or, if the other party is amenable, record your conversation. You are asking for their advice.

• Do not state your case as "fait accompli." Talk about "your approach." Do not ask them to write your memoirs for you since that is your job. You may choose not to take their advice after due reflection, but you will feel better having consulted with them before you publish your memoirs. Talking to them after publication is just bad form.

● ***Do not under any circumstances show your pages to anybody while they are still in draft form.*** Wait until they are completely polished and ready for publication. You will want these people to see only your best work.

● Always remember if you are writing about somebody that you do not like or care for, you must still do it with compassion.

● You can never really know another person's motives. You may guess at them, but make sure your readers know it is your speculation. You should really only be focusing on your own thoughts and motives.

● If you are writing about someone whose opinion is totally opposite to yours, you can are free to just mention it in passing without feeling obliged to fully represent it. You are not obliged to give all sides equal time. This is not a debate. Be truthful and fair, but this memoir is about you. Do not treat this as an essay or dissertation. Long drawn-out debates among your characters will cause your readers to nod off.

● When describing people, avoid jargon. Bob may be a drug addict but don't call him that. Show how his behavior affected you. Talk about anything you did that might have had an impact on him. Give information in the form that you received it. You didn't look at him one day and say, "Bob is a drug addict." Something in his actions and behavior led you to discover that; e.g., "Bob's lapses of memory (consider showing examples) and long absences from work (consider being specific when referring to those absences) were beginning to concern me."

- If you are writing about a very close friend and are writing material of a very sensitive nature; e.g., the death of a loved one, a lost child or sibling or traumatic event, consider sitting with him or her while the pages that are painful are being shared (same house, possibly, but not in the same room). Just being available may help.

- Remove anything that someone denies categorically. Although, truthfully, in most families, the worst stuff was admitted long before you even started writing.

- <u>Always be honest</u>. Honesty must always be your bottom-line. Your memory may be faulty, but you have the right to remember what you remember. Your truth is sometimes bigger than the "facts."

- Honesty in writing your memoir stories means telling the truth of your life experiences and not dressing up those stories with vagueness, exaggeration, or innuendo. It means not telling lies to protect other people or using silence to avoid the truth. Honesty also does not give you license to be brutal and hateful toward other people. You have the right to speak and to tell what you have experienced. You do not have to protect others at the expense of your own truth, but you are not there to blame or point fingers.

- Don't become judgemental and preachy. I know it is sometimes cathartic to be righteous, but in a memoir setting, it wears a little thin. If you find yourself shaking a finger at someone, this may be a sign that you have gone too far.

● As you tell your own stories, you claim your own truth, accept responsibility for your own actions and make sense of the actions of others in the context of your stories.

What Will Others Think?

What happens if you spend your time asking yourself, "What will my sister think?" What is the impact if you keep saying to yourself, "I don't want to hurt anyone?" Or, if you keep worrying that you might get sued, then you need to really stop and give yourself a shake.

Your sister will think what she will think, no matter what you write. And, if she really thinks it happened in a different way, then she can write her own story.

If you write with balance, compassion, integrity, and honesty, you won't hurt anyone. If you are worrying about being sued, first you need a manuscript, and then you can worry about what it contains. That can be discussed in the editing process.

If you worry about these issues before you even start writing, then you are giving yourself permission to stop writing. You will never finish your memoir.

The first draft is just that: a first draft, and it is **your** first draft. Unless you use that first draft to publicly and actively attack, defame, and cause harm or damages to those whom you have written about, you can't be sued.

My advice is to never hold a press conference based on a first draft. Always consider sober second thoughts before publication. Sober second thoughts involve considering what you have written from everybody's viewpoint, not just your own, and then let the editing begin. Don't let the first draft be leaked, lost, or stolen. You don't want to be reading about your unpublished manuscript on "wiki leaks."

In all seriousness, apply due care and attention to the safekeeping and security of your first draft. As they say in the game of bridge, "Breast your cards, dear." There will be ample time to show your hand at the appropriate time.

Chapter 7

The Structure of

Your Memoir

*The real difference between telling what
happened and telling a story about what
happened is that instead of being a victim
of our past, we become a master of it ...
we can't change our past, but we can
change where we stand when we look at it.*
                                        Donald Davis

Just as there are many types of fiction or poetry there
are many "types" or "subgenres" of memoirs; e.g., travel, grief,
family, recovery, romance, or working life.

However, don't worry about your memoir type until you
have started writing your stories. In the beginning you are
finding your own "voice" just as actors or singers find their
niche. You will find yours; or rather, you will develop yours.
Remember, memoirs are not written in a day. Everyone is
different so don't saddle yourself with someone else's mistakes.

Once you start writing your stories and accumulate a number of them, then it will be time to decide what direction you want your memoir to take. You may have decided when you wrote your Mission Statement what your memoir theme would be, but leave yourself open to the possibility of change — or even to the possibility that you may have more than one memoir to write.

Once you start writing the stories, you do not have to write them in order, but I suggest that you print them and lay them out. You will begin to notice a visual picture or map where the stories intersect and perhaps even join together to become one story. You will also start to see patterns emerging from your stories.

You may also discover more than one theme. At some point you will have a decision to make. Are you going to publish more than one memoir or one memoir with several parts? Can you establish a linkage between the parts? Or perhaps, you may write about your business life separately from your coming-of-age years.

Until the stories that are most vivid in your mind are actually put onto paper, you can't even begin to make these decisions. I often hear my students say, "I have already written it in my mind."

Just as there is a difference between oral speech and the printed word, there is a vast difference between thinking a story and the translation of those thoughts onto the printed page. Perhaps thinking a story would be good enough if we could telepathically convey our stories. Maybe in the future, but for the time being you need to get those thoughts onto paper.

How Will I Present My Stories?

Once you have decided on the basic theme that you intend to follow for your memoir, you have to answer the next question: "In what order will I present my stories?" You will have several choices and your answer(s) will depend on exactly what you are trying to tell people about yourself.

For instance, you might consider a **chronological order** which means in order by time; i.e., the order in which the events happened. Perhaps you are doing a travel memoir of the trip you took when you walked the El Camino. You will likely want to start at the beginning of your walk or when you first decided to hike that trail over the Pyrenees from France to Spain. After all, I am sure the decision was not one a person took without considered forethought. However, the number of people who develop debilitating blisters en route may make me reconsider how much forethought was there.

Each of the stories will have to be linked since the reader is looking for "causality" as you move from one challenge to the next or from one decision to the next.

The reader will, of course, be expecting a change of pace or the stories will become monotonous. Clarity and simplicity and a little bit of humor are hard to beat as pace changers. The reader also likes "the unexpected" as it helps break the story into "chunks" that differentiate one section of the story from another.

And remember, you don't have to write the stories in order, even though you will present them in **chronological order** in the final draft.

In the "old days" some writers would write a story and use clothespins to pin it to a clothesline strung up in their office. As each story was written it was added to the line. The writers would then add, delete, and rearrange the stories until they were happy with the order.

My office is much too small to do that, so I store my stories in a file folder and sort them on the floor of the living room. But I must tell you, I always liked the imagery of the writer bent over a typewriter surrounded with his or her stories fluttering on a clothesline in the light breeze from the open window.

Sigh, I think I need to talk to my husband about a bigger office, but in the meantime, it is the file folder and the floor for me.

"And you?" I digress. Time to bring things back to order.

There is also an order called **semi- or anti-chronological.** It is a non-linear structure where you tell the stories in a fragmented manner. This helps to break up what I call "The Never-Ending Story" that drones on and on, one baby step in front of another.

Sometimes you might even stop to talk directly to your readers or meditate (write a mini essay) for a whole chapter or two (as long as it is interesting and germane to your story). If you are going to use this structure, it is best to use a plan or outline; otherwise you may quickly lose your way.

This approach requires you to use flashbacks and flash-forwards. If you use them, consider using them sparingly and, if you do, be very clear about where you are in your timeline. Thinking of these vignettes as scenes in a movie may be helpful. You are the director and it is your job to make sure the overall timeline you are establishing in your story is not lost or broken.

If you confuse your readers, they become upset and quit reading. Even something so simple as providing a date and/or time at the start of a new chapter helps readers keep things straight.

Keep in mind that e-book readers often find flashbacks and flash-forwards very difficult to deal with since paging back and forth through their e-books is not an easy task. Readers of hard-copy books find it easier to go back a few pages to refresh their understanding of the story. Not so easy with an e-book.

An **episodic** structure requires a great deal of planning on your part. Smaller incidents (stories) when taken together form a larger work. Each story becomes an episode in the larger story with its own beginning, middle, and end. W.O. Mitchell's *Jake and the Kid* and James Herriot's *All Creatures Great and Small* spring to mind as examples of this approach to writing.

Each episode has its own narrative or dramatic arc, including a climax of some sort, although it is nowhere as strong as the main story's dramatic arc and climax. Think of a TV series that you enjoy watching. Each episode stands alone, but there is likely an overarching story of some sort that continues for the entire season (or series). It may even end in a cliff hanger which will encourage you to come back for the next season to see what happens. Your next memoir, perhaps?

The **episodic** structure adds power to a memoir by keeping scenes short and self-contained, and it links multiple scenes together by theme or repeated imagery. This approach also makes it easy for the reader to pick up the book and to put it down. One of my students referred to this approach as a "bathroom reader."

Think about a coming-of-age memoir. You could tell the stories of several events leading up to your final emancipation as an adult. You could then have an overarching theme running about whether or not you will overcome some major challenge that is facing you. How did you become of age?

For instance, do you get the scholarship to that big-name university you were working so hard to achieve? Do you marry the woman you have secretly loved all of your life? Life's journeys are endless...

Memoirs using the **episodic** form can feel structurally right even if you play around with the concept of time. If the episodes are compelling, you may even be able to order them any way you choose. I do recommend, however, ensuring each episode interacts with the one immediately before and after it; otherwise you just have a collection of short stories. Short-story authors do spend a lot of time considering the order of their stories because they want to start on a high note and end on a high note.

Thematic Structure

Once you have looked at your collection of stories, you also need to consider if you are going to explore a theme that will lead to an unconventional structure; e.g., my life's story as told through my baking recipes.

Unconventional structures will only work if your theme is well developed, deeply considered, and worthy of a book-length exploration. Using any unconventional structure is tricky and truly depends on what you want to communicate to the reader. In my experience, new writers like the comfort that conventional techniques provide. Having said that, the more adventuresome need to consider the following if they are headed down an unconventional or thematic route.

You have to know your answers to your thematic questions before you even start to order things. Two examples that I have read and are worth reading which follow an unconventional structure are *A Year of Magical Thinking* by Joan Didion and *On Writing: A Memoir of the Craft* by Stephen King.

Some unconventional structures include the following suggestions:

- Cookbooks
- To-do lists
- Catalogs
- Postcards
- Letters
- E-mails, text messages, blog posts
- Photographs
- Songs
- Top Ten Lists
- Diary Entries

Here are a few examples of some of the different varieties of memoirs you might consider writing (but, of course, your memoir will be completely based on your own life experiences—no fiction or experiential plagiarisms in your memoir, please):

- **Relationship** (e.g., *Eat, Pray, Love* by Elizabeth Gilbert)
- **Animal** (e.g., *Marley and Me,* by John Grogan)
- **Illness** (e.g., *When Breath Becomes Air* by Paul Kalanithi)
- **Religious or Spiritual** (e.g., *The Spiral Staircase* by Karen Armstrong)
- **Business** (e.g., *Lean-in* by Sheryl Sandberg)
- **Travel** (e.g., *What the Psychic Told the Pilgrim* by Jane Christmas)
- **Coming-of-age** (e.g., *The Road from Coorain* by Jill Ker Conway)

Of course, if you have time; and, my advice to you is that it would be beneficial to make the time, read a few memoirs written by other people. I have provided a list of excellent memoirs in Appendix II. If you find one or two that appeal to you, read those memoirs. All you have to lose is the time you spend learning from others. Remember, you are reading to learn and you must demonstrate that learning through your own writing. After all, this is a writing exercise and not a reading exercise.

So now you have structural choices in a nutshell: chronological, semi- or anti-chronological, episodic, thematic, or even no specific structure at all. You will have to choose the one that most suits your writing style and the theme of your memoir.

But don't rush to choose. Wait until you've written enough stories that you begin to get a sense of where you are going. When I first started, I thought I was going to write a memoir about traveling with my husband–the good times, the bad times, the fun times, and the funny times; but as I began to write my stories, the stories from my youth and my growing up years kept jumping to the head of the line. That doesn't mean those "Traveling with David" stories won't get written, it just means they will likely be in a separate memoir.

That's what I mean by not deciding in advance what direction your memoir is going to take.

Chapter 8

Editing Your Memoirs

The critical, final step after you have rewritten, revised, and done your own manuscript editing is to hire a third party to edit your manuscript—not your aunt who was an English teacher or your neighbor who was an English major in university or your best friend who is going to do it for free.

There may be exceptions, but I see many more failures of a project using a "friend" versus the use of a professional editor. The reason for this is your friends know you or "think" they know you. When they edit your book, they rewrite or edit your book through their eyes; in other words, how they see you. As a result you lose control of your book and rather than disagree with "a respected friend," you quietly give up.

Keep your friends as friends and move forward with an independent editor who is not going to judge you, nor tell you what you did or did not include, nor dictate how you should feel. This is your story; keep it as your story.

There is likely an Editors' Association is your local area. Find them and ask them to recommend someone you can hire. You can also hire an editor on-line. But, please be careful. In the world of on-line editors, you will likely get exactly what you pay for. No matter what editor you hire, always ask for references and do due diligence to make sure the person is a *bone fide* editor.

There are different types of editors and you may choose to have one, two, or three rounds of editing. If you are working with a professional editor, you will be making certain decisions regarding spelling, punctuation, and certain grammar usage prior to the start of the editing process.

A professional editor will provide you with a Style Sheet where he or she will have recorded items such as the spelling used for the names of characters, streets, unusual spellings, and punctuations (such as the use of a serial comma). If you do not receive a Style Sheet, you are not working with a professional editor.

"What types of editors are there?" you ask.

Substantive Editor

The first editor you may choose to work with is a **substantive editor**. A substantive editor does the following tasks:

- Improves sentence construction to more effectively convey meaning (e.g., choosing active voice over passive in most contexts, making unparallel constructions parallel, etc.);

- Improves word choice to more effectively convey meaning (e.g., by replacing the general and abstract with the specific and concrete, eliminating clichés and euphemisms);

- Where necessary, rewrites sentences, paragraphs, and passages to resolve ambiguities, ensure logical connections, and clarify the author's meaning or intention, in harmony with the style of the material;

- Changes as little as possible and attempts to preserve the author's voice where appropriate;

- Ensures that all tables, photos, multimedia, and other visual elements are clear and effectively convey the intended meaning;

- Ensures that transitions between sentences and between paragraphs are smooth and support the coherent development of the text as a whole;

- Where necessary, reorders sentences within a paragraph to ensure the paragraph has a clear and coherent focus;

- Adjusts the length and structure of paragraphs to ensure variety or consistency as appropriate to the audience and medium;

- Adjusts the length and structure of sentences to ensure variety or consistency as appropriate to the audience and medium;

- Determines the language and reading level appropriate for the intended audience and medium, and edits to establish or maintain that language and level;

- Establishes or maintains a consistent tone, style, and authorial voice or level of formality appropriate for the intended audience and medium;

- Eliminates wordiness (e.g., by deleting redundancies, empty phrases, unnecessary modifiers);

- Reorganizes material to achieve a coherent structure and sequence;

- Identifies, and either recommends or makes appropriate deletions and additions in both text and visual elements.

This sounds like a lot, and it is. A substantive editor needs to ensure that the flow of the story is clear and coherent. If editors cannot fulfil their mandate, they will ask that you provide them with additional information or new text to help them fill in the identified gaps. They will not be shy about pointing out gaps in your timelines or ambiguities in your story that stump them. While this is often a humbling experience, it should also be an enlightening one. You will learn things about yourself and your writing that you will never learn from a friend. They are not paid to be your friend; their job is to help you express your thoughts and experiences in a clear and coherent manner in a style that you have chosen for your memoir. They can make suggestions, but in the end, the final decisions are yours.

Copy Editor

At the very least, you should hire a **copy editor.** The copy editor does very specific tasks and does not work at the same depth as a substantive editor. However, copy editors can work more quickly and, as a result, will cost you less money. Most good writers, if they have the resources, will put their manuscripts through both a substantive editor and a copy editor. Please note that these are usually two different people.

The copy editor performs the following tasks:

• Corrects errors in grammar (e.g., lack of subject-verb agreement, misplaced modifiers, and incorrect pronoun case);

• Corrects punctuation errors (e.g., comma splices, misplaced colons, and incorrect apostrophes);

• Corrects errors in spelling (e.g., typographical errors or errors arising from homonyms and similar-sounding words);

• Corrects errors in usage (e.g., words commonly confused, such as imply/infer; incorrect idioms and phrases such as "centers around");

• Identifies categories of editorial style (e.g., abbreviations, measurements, treatment of numbers, or Canadian/British/American spelling);

- Provides you with a style sheet to better understand and track editorial style;

- Identifies, and either corrects or queries inconsistencies in logic, factual details, and cross-references;

- Ensures that all tables, photos, multimedia, and other visual elements are consistent with surrounding text and are consistently presented (e.g., headings, captions, or numbering);

- Understands the issues related to using other languages, especially French or Spanish, in an English context (e.g., capitalization, italicization, or accented characters) and edits for consistency;

- Identifies, and either corrects or queries items that should be checked for accuracy (e.g., names of people and places, titles, quotations, or web links);

- Identifies, and either corrects or queries errors in material containing statistics, mathematics, and numerals (e.g., incorrect imperial/metric conversions, or incorrect totals in tables);

- Ensures that material is complete and, as appropriate, query or supply missing elements (e.g., captions and headings, web links, phone numbers, or addresses);

- Recognizes elements that require copyright acknowledgement and permission to reproduce (e.g., quotations, multimedia, or photos).

- **Please note the following about COPY EDITORS:**

- They are not rewriters or ghost writers. Copy editors can make simple revisions to smooth awkward passages, but they do not have license to write or rewrite text line by line.

- They are not proofreaders. Many copy editors are good proofreaders, but at the copyedit level, they are not expected to catch typographical errors. Copyediting and proofreading are usually two different functions.

- They are not substantive editors. Copy editors can query structural and organizational problems, but they are not expected to fix these problems.

Proofreader

And then you have the **proofreaders**. Do not, under any circumstances, send anything you have written out into the world unless it has been proofread at least once. Twice or three times is probably better. I can't count the number of times that I have read and reread a piece several times, and yet I catch new errors each time I reread it.

When do you stop proofreading? You stop just before you think that you will throw up if you have to read the piece one more time! If you don't proofread a piece, you will have to endure the abuse of your readers who will then take great pride in pointing out all of your grammatical shortcomings and typographical errors. Best to get it right and avoid all the bad press.

Professional proofreaders have their own techniques. However, if you really believe you need to save the money somewhere, do not save it on a copy editor. Save it on the proofreader.

Here is how you do it. You have two copies of your manuscript. You ask one of your dear, close, non-judgemental friends who does not mind being prevailed upon to help you. One of you will read the manuscript <u>out loud</u> while the other silently reads the other manuscript following along word for word with a finger under each word.

Use this technique and you will catch most of the errors between the two of you. Don't rush this process and take frequent rest and/or coffee breaks. Be sure to point out and mark each error as you find it.

You must also read all the punctuation marks and verbally indicate when a new paragraph has started. If you are going to take turns reading out loud, then you must switch manuscripts so that the proofreading marks only go on one manuscript.

You can obtain a set of the "shorthand marks" used by proofreaders on the internet at

http://www.chicagomanualofstyle.org/tools_proof.html

I encourage you to learn and use this shorthand as the proofreaders' marks are quick, unambiguous, and universal among all writers and editors. These marks are one of the valuable tools that are kept in your writer's toolbox.

Once you have completed this process, go and make your edits accordingly. If you can stand it, repeat this exercise with the edited manuscript and preferably with a new friend. A new set of eyes always finds new mistakes. Repeat until your manuscript is error-free or you just can't stand to do it one more time.

I will ask you again: "Are you sure you don't want to hire a professional proofreader?"

Here is what you can expect from a professional proofreader:

• A proofreader adheres to the editorial style sheet that is appropriate for your memoir and will update it if necessary. If no style sheet is provided, the proofreader will prepare one and update it as the proofreading progresses;

• At first-proof stage, the proofreader reads the memoir word by word while comparing it with a second copy (if supplied by you);

• After first proof and on all subsequent proofs, the proofreader refrains from reading the entire text again (unless instructed to do so by you) but will check that all changes have been made as requested and that the new changes do not introduce new problems (e.g., check line- and page-breaks, text flow, table of contents, navigation bar, etc.);

• Sometimes the law of "unintended consequences" rears its ugly head during the edit process and this will need to be addressed before a bad edit turns into a worse problem. My own millstone often comes to light around changes I make in setting margins and making format changes. I change a margin on one page and somehow I inadvertently change a different page that I didn't want changed. I need to be super vigilant about such changes and so should you. A proofreader will keep track of such things;

• At all proof stages, a proofreader will refrain from undertaking structural, stylistic, or copyediting tasks unless authorized to do so by you. Sometimes they will point out a problem but it will be your responsibility to make the changes. By the way, if you ask them to make changes, they will charge you extra for that service. Be careful what you authorise them to do. You do not want to give them *carte blanche* only to find out you disagree with their changes. You will then have to go back and unmake those changes even though you have paid them to make changes "as they saw fit";

• The proofreader ensures that the first proof contains all the elements in the copy prepared for layout (e.g., all paragraphs, visual elements, headings, etc.);

• The proofreader also identifies and corrects typographical and formatting errors, paying special attention to problematic areas (e.g., spelling of proper names and non-English words, accuracy of numbers, tables, and figures);

• A proofreader checks consistency and accuracy of the different elements in the material (e.g., cross-references, running heads, captions, titles of web windows, hyper links, metadata, etc.);

• The proofreader checks end-of-line word divisions and marks bad breaks for your correction;

• A proofreader understands design specifications and ensures that they have been followed throughout (e.g., by checking alignment, type size and style, line length, space around major elements, use of colour, and appearance of hyper links);

• Typographical and formatting irregularities are recognized (e.g., widows and orphans, overly ragged edges, ill-fitting text, and incorrect text colour) and adjustments to eliminate these problems are suggested;

• Matters that may affect later stages of production are flagged for you (e.g., page cross-references, placement of art, and alterations that will change layout, indexing, or web navigation);

• A proofreader will query, or correct, if authorized to do so, inconsistencies (e.g., in spelling, punctuation, fact, visual elements, navigation elements, metadata, or other content that may not appear on a published web page). Professional judgment will also be used about the degree to which such queries and corrections are necessary.

As a final note, most editors work electronically, using Microsoft Word and *"Track Changes"* (an editing feature within the Word Program). If you need to be shown how to use *Track Changes*, I would suggest seeking help from a local continuing education center. Or, if you are comfortable using the internet, there are many instructional articles and videos on-line that will help you learn about *Track Changes*.

Very few editors work from paper or "hard copy" any longer and those who do will charge you considerably more money than those who work electronically. Learning how to effectively use *Track Changes* will make your editing experience far easier and less expensive as well as increase the selection of editors available to you. Editors will then also communicate with you via e-mail; which is faster and more efficient. It is not difficult to learn *Track Changes*, and the payback is huge. Be at one with your editor(s).

Chapter 9

Summing it All Up

Why Memoirs Fail

Taking into account all the things I have been telling you and showing you in this book, you need to be aware of the most common reasons about why memoirs fail. I am not only talking about books written about a specific memoir topic such as an adventure story, a survival story, a family triumph, or tragedy story, but I am also talking about the shorter stories we write and don't use.

You think these shorter stories may still someday be included in a book of short stories for your family or be published for the wider public to read; or maybe you intend to write stories about your working life or your political life, but for the moment, you are stalled. The secret of getting started again is to understand why you have stalled and why others fail.

How disappointing would it be after spending all that time writing, crafting, honing, and polishing your stories, your book(s) were only met with criticism? What if no one actually read them with the enthusiasm you anticipated? What do you think could have gone wrong?

Let's look at some of the more critical errors that the writers of memoir and memoir stories make.

Insufficient Editing

Please do not ask your favorite aunt or your next-door neighbor (who does or does not have a degree in English) to be your editor. Don't ask your wife or your husband to be your editor (even if he or she was a teacher of English). You need a third party, unrelated to you and preferably not a good friend or acquaintance to act as your editor. Someone who is competent, will see the story as you wrote it, and will not try to filter it through his or her own biases. This is your story, not that of your friend or relative.

If you are going to spend money printing your book (or even taking the time to publish it as an e-book), make sure it is as good as you can make it. You spent all that time writing it. Have it properly edited. When you hand your book to readers and you apologize to them that you missed a few errors in the editing or proofreading, they won't be inclined to spend their valuable time reading a book you did not have the time or respect for them, as the reader, to ensure it was correct before you published it. You will get unenthusiastic feedback which you will translate into failure and disappointment. You can avoid this pitfall by taking the time and making the effort to get it right.

Some writers love the editing process and others hate it. If you fall into the latter category, you really need the help of a professional editor to bring your book to a satisfactory conclusion.

Often new writers don't seek the help of an outside editor because their friends and relatives talk them out of it. These well-intentioned advisors are not writers, and they don't understand the important role editors play in the writing process.

Editors may work behind the scenes but I can tell you that in the acknowledgment section of many books you pick up there is a "thank you" to the editors. Why? Because editors do what writers cannot.

The story is yours. Editors only assist you with the telling. Chances are that you take your car to a mechanic for repair and maintenance. The mechanic does not tell you where to drive; they just help you get to where you want to go. Think of your editor as your "writing mechanic."

Data Dumping vs. Storytelling

The first chapters of some memoirs are fact-packed dreary affairs. They read more like autobiographies than memoirs. These memoirs remind me of slogging through muskeg and having to jump from one hummock to another without sinking into the mire. Sooner or later you know you will fall and it will not be a pretty sight. Imparting background information to your readers need not be painful.

Remember informational writing just "tells"; writing by "showing" will allow the reader a better opportunity to see your story as you experienced it. Excessive telling or listing of information pulls the reader away from the action and drama of the story. Or, it may take far too long for the story to even start if the writer feels compelled to fill the reader full of back story and facts before even starting the real story.

When this happens, most readers feel like they have returned to school where the "old school marm" is up there in front of the class spouting the day's lesson through the recitation of dry facts and figures. Show your readers the story; don't just tell them the facts.

Lacking Focus

If there is no conflict, there is no story. If there is no story, the reader gets bored, loses interest, and quits reading. Failure is assured.

Skipping or Avoiding the Most Interesting or Juiciest Parts

Shallow writing usually stems from a lack of "psychological self-knowledge"; i.e., the writer does not have or is not willing to share enough information to adequately inform the reader what the story is, or there may be a lack of willingness to tell the truth.

If the narrator is always portrayed as tough or stoical or self-sacrificing or always ready with the quick quip or smartass posture, then that character lacks depth and believability. Such characters are hackneyed and predictable. Life is broad-reaching and when portrayed as narrow, the portrayal is not believable and the story fails.

Avoiding what the reader knows to be the real issue or the real story makes the reader know that the writer is not being honest and truthful in writing the memoir. A dishonest memoir is worse than not having written any memoir at all.

Moving at an Incredibly...Slow...Pace

If you move too quickly over the dramatic events and then s..l..o..w to a snail's pace over banal information and then head off on a marginally related tangent, you will try a reader's patience to exhaustion.

You want to build anticipation but not tease the reader into boredom. Bad pacing is often a sign that the writer does not have a plan in mind or an outline to follow; i.e., the writer is lost and disorganized. Lack of planning will ensure failure.

Failing to Offer a True Emotional Experience

You must meet the readers where they are by offering information in a way that is "felt," and you must reflect your inner values and cares realistically through the stories that you write.

I know that this is easier said than done, but the readers will see right through the portrayal of false emotion and inappropriate behavior. Memoirs need to be believable and, to be believable, your story needs to be honestly portrayed and that includes emotional responses.

Bludgeoning Readers with Your Theme

Do not tell the readers what they should think or feel. Just tell them the story. They will form their own opinions about how they feel and what is important in your story. You should never use the words, "...and the moral of the story is..."

And do not try to think up clever little ways to say that same thing using different words. If your story has a message that you want the readers to absorb, they will "get it" if the story is well told.

The most poorly written memoir, in my opinion, depicts a bitter story that is nothing more than a vengeful tell-all. Most of these bitter stories are, quite frankly, unreadable. Write a vengeful tirade as a cathartic exercise if you must, but think twice before you make it public.

If you feel that you have been wronged in some way, tell your story in a manner that shows you rising above adversity as opposed to being consumed by victim madness.

Overcomplicating the Story

If you have too many characters with confusing or similar names or if the plot is intricate and changes location frequently, then the reader is forced to keep flipping back and forth to sort out the plot and the characters—sometimes even the timeline. This stops the smooth flow of the reading and can be even more difficult if the reader is using an e-book. It is like watching a movie where the actors look alike, dress alike, and have the same look and mannerisms; the viewer is unable to follow the plot and the movie bombs. Memoirs are no different.

In a short story, the "rule-of-thumb" used by many storytellers is to keep it to no more than three characters. In a written story, as opposed to an oral story, you may be able to expand that to four or five characters, but definitely no more. If you need a cast of a thousand to support your story, you may need to write more than a single memoir. Too much of anything is just too much to take in.

Writing with Mere Competence

Bad sentences make bad paragraphs, and bad paragraphs make bad memoirs. Competent writers write clearly, logically, and compellingly. They are effective in getting their readers to read and understand their stories.

To achieve this goal, writers need to revise, review, and revise again if that is what it takes. Revisions are about writing clear sentences and ensuring that you are evoking the same emotions in the reader that were once evoked in you.

As an aside, don't forget, your character has to change over time just as you changed. If you have characters that don't change over time or who lack depth, they become predictable and then you may only have a portrait and not a story.

Why Memoirs Succeed

You Practiced, Practiced, Practiced

You wrote your stories until you had many, many stories that were important to you. Practice gave you confidence as well as allowed you to try different approaches to writing.

I have heard it said that you should write away and then throw away those first hundred pages as practice pages. I personally think that you should revise and edit those first hundred pages; don't throw them away, just make them better!

The more you write the more you will know how to write. But, remember it is a multistage process. Write, revise, and edit; that's the secret path, and you must practice <u>each of these steps</u> in order to be a successful writer.

You Waited to Choose Your Theme

After taking the time to write your many stories, you stopped and looked at what you had written. A period of thoughtful reflection can be invaluable to the writing process. You saw what topics were important to you, identified what stories you needed to tell, and then eliminated or cast aside others.

At that moment you decided what the shape of your memoir(s) would be. You then took the stories you had written and combined some, rearranged the order, revised them, rewrote them, and wrote others to fill in the missing pieces.

Sometimes this came together in a flash and sometimes it happened only after you had a debate with your inner self. Me? I like to make lists and see visually what I have done and then I can better envision where I should be going. No matter how you go about doing your thoughtful reflection, there is one question I am sure that you are going to ask yourself.

"Why have I waited so long to do this?" Yes, you have worked hard and it has taken you a while to get where you are now, but "How long did you just 'think' about writing your memoir versus the time that it actually took you to write it?" That's the difference between thinking about doing something versus actually doing it.

Mark Twain said "The secret of getting ahead is getting started." He also went on to say "The secret of getting started is breaking your complex, overwhelming tasks into small manageable tasks, then starting on the first one." Sound familiar? That's what successful writers do. That's what you did.

Your Story is the Right Length

A successful writer doesn't feel the need to pad the memoir with stories that are only being used to fill pages and make the book thicker. As a successful memoir writer you have included only stories that were important to you and to the theme that you have chosen. I would rather read a short, well written story than a long, trivial piece of drivel. Wouldn't you?

Often I am asked, "How long should a story be?" My quick answer is, "As long as it needs to be." Here is a short story consisting of 6 words that is attributed to Ernest Hemingway. Does it need to be longer to evoke emotion from the reader?

> *For sale:*
> *baby shoes,*
> *never worn.*

You Used an Editor

Most successful memoir authors hired a professional editor. It could have been a substantive editor, a copy editor, and/or a proofreader. At the very least, you hired a copy editor and proofread your document word-by-word with another person reading one copy while you read the other copy out loud.

One of the reasons why editors are so important to memoir writers is that memoir writers rarely have a lot of experience writing and the mechanics of writing eludes them. I think that in memoir writing, it is the story that is important and not the mechanics of writing. Don't get hung up by the mechanics of the writing process. The editors can't tell your story for you because they don't know your story, but they can help you with the mechanics of the process. Together you will make "sweet" stories.

You Found the Human Connection

Successful writers connect the reader to the people in the stories and not just to events. As a successful memoir writer you connected your readers to your feelings about the events that transpired and your readers realized how those events changed you; they now understand you. Further, you wrote as if you were talking—as if you were telling or showing your story to your family or friends while sitting around a coffee table, a dinner table, or a campfire. Your story was not forced down the reader's throat. You led them through your journey as willing and interested participants. And, you left them wanting more...

You Wrote Complete Stories

Successful memoir writers follow the time-honored tradition of writing stories with a beginning, middle, and an end. As a successful writer you used plot models like "The Hero's Journey" or "Freytag's Pyramid" to help guide you with the telling of your story.

You did not just write portraits of people you once knew or essays about what you "think" or rather "thought" about an event. You wrote stories that had a plot which was told using similes and metaphors while guiding your reader from the beginning to the end of your story(ies).

You Took Pride in your Memoir

Successful writers take pride in their work. As a successful memoir writer you took pride in your work. You took the initiative and found the fortitude to tell your story. Do not sell yourself short.

How many people talk about writing their memoir and how many actually do it? Sure, some people will love your memoir and some will hate it while others may be indifferent. That is not the point.

You felt that your story needed to be told and you succeeded. The memoir is like a child that receives unconditional love from its mother. You bore it, be proud of what you did. That is not to say you can't create more memoirs just as you can always have more children; figuratively speaking, that is.

As with children, you will be asked which memoir you love best. The answer is that you love them all, but your last one is always special. As the eldest child, I hate that answer, but as a writer, I love it.

Epilogue

You are now ready to start writing your memoir in earnest. You have done your practice writing. Your Memory List has grown exponentially, and you have a good idea which stories you want to start writing. You may or may not have decided on a theme or a structure for the final memoir. You may or may not have decided if, in fact, you are going to divide your memoirs into several different books. You just know that you are going to start writing.

Your writing schedule is firmly in place. You have committed to this project and you know you want to do your best to make it happen. File folders, binders, computer space are all organized and at the ready, waiting for you to begin writing.

You now start to turn down coffee dates and other activities if people try to schedule them during your writing time. You ask them if they are available at other times. You would still like to enjoy their company, just not during the time you have now set aside as your writing time.

When they ask you why you can't come for coffee at that time or on that day any more like you used to, you finally 'fess up.

"I'm writing my memoirs," you say.

"Really? What are they about?"

Are you ready to answer that question?

If not, take the time right now and prepare your answer. Or better yet, prepare several answers.

You will need the 30-second answer for the person who was just asking the polite question and really couldn't care less.

You will need the one- to two-minute answer for the friend who is actually interested, but doesn't have a lot of time at that point to talk to you.

And finally, you will need the five-minute answer for the good friend who is very interested and really wants to have that cup of coffee and understand what you are doing with that time you are protecting so carefully.

These are the equivalent of the short resumés you might have had to do if you were looking for work at a job fair.

The 30-second answer was similar to the "elevator" pitch about yourself. You were supposed to sell yourself, to tell your best qualities in the time it took for the elevator to arrive or in the time it took to ride up in the elevator with the person you were trying to impress.

The one- to two-minute answer was the "pitch" you would make to the potential employer at the booth at the job fair. The five-minute answer was the one you used if you were invited into the booth to sit down and talk to the personnel agent in a little more depth about yourself. Or, it was the answer to the question at the job interview, "Why should we hire you for this job?"

If you don't have your three answers ready <u>and rehearsed</u>, you will just stumble around looking for a way to explain what you are doing. The impression will be that you are not really writing your memoirs, you're probably just surfing the web and really don't want to be interrupted.

You need to sound confident and certain. You need to sound like you have a plan, that you have thought this over, and you know what you want to write about.

You don't have to reveal all the details of what you are writing. You never have to reveal details until you are ready to do so, but if you can give some general idea what you are doing, then the people who are interested will be very supportive. They need to feel your enthusiasm and believe in your own dedication to your own project.

Now, sit down and write your stories.

Write with joy!

Marva K. Blackmore

Appendices

Appendix I

Memoir Writing Groups

If you plan to form a Memoir Writing Group, this is a good idea. These groups motivate people to keep going and to get feedback from those who wish to share their individual stories. Those stories, of course, may or may not be included in the final memoir, but it gives each person a chance to read a story out loud and to ask for and receive feedback from the group.

The ideal size of a group varies. It will depend on how long you intend to meet (one, two, or three hours) and how long you want to allot for each person to read and receive feedback. For instance, if a person were to read for no more than 10 minutes (about 3-4 pages) and receive feedback for 10 minutes, then at 20 minutes per person, three people per hour could be accommodated.

The other important issue is confidentiality. The group needs to agree in advance that everything read and heard in the group is confidential and must not be repeated outside the group. First, there may be sensitive issues discussed in a person's writing and second, many writers do not want their stories made public before they choose to make them public themselves.

The membership of this group should remain fixed and stable. You might consider starting out with a slightly larger number knowing that you will have some attrition. However, after a certain point, you should agree that no new members can be added to the group without the agreement of all members. Usually if the group becomes too small due to attrition, then the group may decide to disband and re-form as another group incorporating new members rather than just adding members.

Some groups choose to circulate copies of their writing in advance so others can make notes to give back to the writer. Some choose to bring a copy for each member at the meeting. Other groups simply read their stories to each other.

Every group should have a facilitator who acts as the timekeeper for the meeting. This role should rotate. It can be as simple as having the timekeeper be the person who is hosting if the group moves from house to house. However the group chooses to function and meet, the facilitator role should be determined at the end of the meeting for the following meeting.

Also, each person should provide his or her feedback (consider going around in a circle) before any general discussion takes place. Authors should not be tempted to jump in, but should wait and listen until everyone has spoken. If discussion is desirable, it should take place after everyone has had a chance to speak.

At first, authors have a tendency to "defend" themselves against all comers. It may take a few sessions for everyone to feel comfortable enough with the process to "hear" the comments and decide whether or not they want to take those comments under consideration. This is not meant to be a confrontational process. As an author, just listen and learn. The authors can take notes if they like.

The author does not respond to the general comments made by others, but just listens. Do not address direct questions to the author. He or she will learn more from listening to the discussion of the other members about the work than from responding to questions or clarifying things for them.

Here are some guidelines for giving and receiving feedback in a Memoir Writing Group.

When Your Work is Being Discussed

- Do not explain your intentions about the writing. Just read it. If it works, your intentions will be clear.

- Do not tell exactly when, where, or how you wrote the piece. This is not relevant.

- Do not respond *at all until everyone* has commented. You are to remain silent throughout the feedback; just listen.

- Do ask for the specific feedback you would like (i.e., is the picture of my mother clear?)

- Do make notes on your copy as people talk — even if you don't agree with what they say.

When Someone Else's Work is Being Discussed

- Do not offer criticism in a way that makes the author feel stupid or insulted. Be respectful.

- Do not make sweeping judgments ("This is good" or "This is bad"). Give your responses using the pronoun "I" ("I was moved by the last section" or "I was confused when you changed locations").

- Do not tell stories from your own experience when discussing the work of another author. This is not about you; it is about the author's writing.

- Do not assume that an "I" character in the story is the author sitting before you. Even if the writing is a memoir, refer to the "I" character in the memoir as "the speaker" or "the narrator." The process becomes too confusing or personal when the author is addressed as "you" by the reviewers when referring to the character in the book. In other words couch your comments in the memoir. Treat the real life author and the character in the book as two separate identities.

- Do not try to make major changes to another participant's stories, reword the story in your own words, or impose your own view. Make general suggestions for consideration, but do not do the writing for the author.

- Do not expound on a point of view that has already been clearly made by someone else. You can say you agree or simply pass on that point.

- Do articulate your response as clearly as you can. It is not enough to simply "feel" something or talk in generalities.

- Do tell the author what you liked, what moved you, and what you can still see or feel after listening to the story. (These positive responses should come first.)

- Do tell the author what you remember most clearly and what had an impact on you.

- Do tell the author where you lost attention or were confused.

- Do write notes on your copy of the work if you like and give it back to the author at the end of the session. This is particularly useful for grammar, punctuation, and spelling corrections.

Memoir groups are helpful because you learn from each other as well as provide motivational support. You understand what each other is going through and are able to relate to successes as well as failures.

It is not that misery loves company, but rather that hard workers rejoice in each other's company.

Appendix II

Suggested Memoir Reading

Memoirs Worth Reading

Maya Angelou, *I Know Why the Caged Bird Sings*

Russell Baker, *Growing Up*

Ishmael Beah, *A Long Way Gone*

Augusten Burroughs, *Running with Scissors: A Memoir*

Joan Didion, *The Year of Magical Thinking*

Annie Dillard, *An American Childhood*

David Eggers, *A Heartbreaking Work of Staggering Genius*

Lucy Grealy, *Autobiography of a Face*

Patricia Hampl, *The Florist's Daughter*

Maxine Hong Kingston, *The Warrior Woman*

Mary Karr, *The Liars' Club*

Susanna Kaysen, *Girl, Interrupted*

Garrison Keillor, *Lake Woebegon Days*

Jon Krakauer, *Into Thin Air*

Jill Ker Conway, *The Road from Coorain*

Ben Logan, *This Land Remembers*

Mary McCarthy, *Memories of a Catholic Girlhood*

Ann Patchett, *Truth & Beauty*

Jeannette Walls, *The Glass Castle*

Eudora Welty, *One Writer's Beginnings*

Tobias Wolff, *This Boy's Life*

Books on Writing and Memoir Writing

Kerry Cohen: *The Truth of Memoir*

> How to write about yourself and others with honesty, emotion, and integrity.

Stephen King: *On Writing: A Memoir of the Craft*

> Whether or not you read his fiction, this book offers good, solid advice and a great story.

Anne Lamott, *Bird by Bird*

> Insights in to a writer's life and includes encouraging fast-paced instructions

Bill Roorbach, *Writing Life Stories*

> If you are looking for a longer list of memoirs to read, he has an extensive list of possibilities.

William Strunk & E. B. White, *The Elements of Style*

> This timeless book is likely on your shelf. If not, check out the next used book sale. Buy it, study it, enjoy it. It's worth it the time you spend with it.

Vogler, Christopher, *The Writer's Journey*

> If you would like to have a fuller understanding of "The Hero's Journey," this is the best book to read to understand the intricacies of this mythic structure.

William Zinsser, *Inventing the Truth: The Art and Craft of Memoir*

> Zinsser and other contributors offer advice on the task of writing about your life.

William Zinsser, *On Writing Well*

> If you are going to read only one book on writing, read this one.

Appendix III

World Events

A Short Synopsis of World Events from 1900 to the Early 21st Century

These are events that made the news and are meant to highlight what was happening in our world around that time.

These events are to help you establish a timeline against which your stories can be anchored.

They are also listed here to help you ask yourself questions as you prepare stories from your Memory List.

Were you alive when the Berlin Airlift took place? Did your parents or grandparents talk about events that took place during World War II or post-war that you remember vividly?

Did you watch The Ed Sullivan Show when the Beatles appeared? Elvis Presley? Or even some other entertainer that made an impression on you?

There are some events that become imprinted on the "national" psyche. What were you doing when you heard that Kennedy was shot? When Neil Armstrong walked on the moon? Or when the Challenger space shuttle blew up?

Did you go to Woodstock? Did you have friends who went? Did you watch it on TV and wonder about it? Did you buy the record and listen to it over and over? Memorize some of the songs? What did the whole experience mean to you?

What about the day Princess Diana was killed? The day the Twin Towers came down?

We all share a common history. It is our reactions to that history and our stories of those reactions that are interesting and worth exploring for ourselves and for our families.

1900-1909

1900	Kodak introduces the $1 Brownie camera
1901	Queen Victoria dies
	Marconi sends radio broadcast over ocean
1902	Boer War ends
1903	Wright Brothers first flight
1904	Work commences on the Panama Canal
1905	Theory of Relativity published by Einstein
	Alberta and Saskatchewan join Canada
1906	San Francisco earthquake
1907	First electric washing machine
1908	Model T Ford introduced
	Boy Scout movement founded by Baden Powell
	Lucy Maud Montgomery writes Anne of Green Gables
1909	Plastic invented

1910-1919

1910	Haley's Comet appears
1912	Sinking of the Titanic
1914	Panama Canal opens

1914	World War I begins
1917	Bolshevik Revolution in Russia
	The Halifax munitions explosion
1918	Tsar Nicholas and family assassinated
	World War I ends
1919	The atom is split
	Treaty of Versailles

1920-1929

1920	League of Nations established
1922	Insulin discovered by Banting & Best
1923	Time Magazine founded
1924	First Winter Olympic Games
1925	Robert Goddard fires the first liquid fuel rocket
1927	First talking movie (The Jazz Singer)
	Lindbergh flies from New York to Paris
1928	Alexander Fleming discovers penicillin
	Bubble gum invented
1929	October crash of the New York stock market
	Car radio invented

1930-1939

1930	Pluto discovered
1931	Empire State Building completed
1932	Air conditioning invented
1933	Hitler becomes Germany's Chancellor
	FDR launches the New Deal
1934	Dionne quintuplets born (first to survive in world)
	The Dust Bowl
	Monopoly was created
1934	The cheeseburger was created
1935	Radar invented

1935	AA founded
1936	Spanish Civil War begins
	Berlin Summer Olympics
1937	Hindenburg disaster
1938	Hitler annexes Austria
1939	First jet aircraft invented
	Helicopter invented
	World War II begins
	Spanish Civil War ends

1940-1949

1940	Battle of Britain
	Trotsky assassinated
1941	Japanese attack Pearl Harbor
	Jeep invented
1942	First nuclear reactor
	T-shirt introduced
1943	Warsaw Ghetto uprising
1944	Ballpoint pens go on sale
	D-Day invasion
1945	World War II ends
	First computer (ENIAC) built
1946	UN General Assembly meets
	Bikinis introduced
	Nuremburg Trials
1947	Medicare first brought into Saskatchewan
	Dead Sea Scrolls discovered
	Polaroid camera invented
1947	First supersonic aircraft
	Transistor invented
1949	Newfoundland joins Canada

1949	NATO founded
	Berlin airlift
	Israel founded

1950-1959

1950	Korean War begins
	First Peanuts cartoon
	Modern credit card introduced
	Early TV in black and white
	Early tape recorders
1952	First color TV
	Elizabeth II becomes Queen
1953	Mount Everest climbed
	DNA structure discovered
	Stalin dies
	Playboy magazine published
1954	Bannister breaks 4-minute mile
	First atomic submarine
1955	Hovercraft invented
	Disneyland opens
	Rosa Parks refuses to give up her seat on the bus
1956	Suez Canal crisis
	Elvis is seen on the Ed Sullivan Show
	TV remote control invented
1957	Russian Sputnik 1 launched
1958	Hula hoops are all the rage
1959	St. Lawrence Seaway opened
	Castro becomes dictator of Cuba

1960-1969

| 1960 | Lasers invented |

1961	First man in space (Russian Yuri Gagarin)
	Berlin wall built
1962	Cuban missile crisis
1963	U.S. President Kennedy assassinated
1964	Beatles on the Ed Sullivan Show
1965	U.S. troops move into South Vietnam
1966	Star Trek series airs
	Cultural Revolution launched in China
1967	First successful human heart transplant
	Arab-Israeli "Six-Day War"
	National Medicare begins in Canada
1968	Martin Luther King Jr. assassinated
	Robert F. Kennedy assassinated
	Tet Offensive in Vietnam
	Prague Spring
1969	Supersonic passenger aircraft
	Apollo 11 lands on moon
	Woodstock
	Sesame Street first airs

1970-1979

1970	Boeing's 747 Jumbo Jet
	U.S. troops leave Vietnam
	Kent State massacre
	Apollo 13 mission
	Beatles break up
1970	Floppy disks introduced
1971	VCR introduced
1972	Nixon visits China
	Munich Olympics
1973	Yom Kippur War

1974	Watergate cover-up
	President Richard Nixon resigns
1977	Montreal Olympics
	Elvis Presley dies
1978	First 'test tube baby' born in UK
1979	Three-Mile Island nuclear event
	Mount St. Helens erupts in U.S.
	USSR invades Afghanistan

1980-1989

1980	Iran hostage incident begins
	Moscow Olympics
1981	US space shuttle with Canadarm
	IBM sells 1st Personal Computer
1982	Falklands invaded by Britain
	Michael Jackson releases Thriller album
1983	Cabbage Patch dolls become popular
1984	First Macintosh computer released
	Indira Ghandi assassinated
1985	New Coke hits the market
	Titanic found
1986	Space Shuttle Challenger blows up on take off
	Chernobyl nuclear disaster in USSR
1987	World stock market crash
	Calgary Winter Olympics
1987	DNA used to convict criminals for the first time
1989	Tiananmen Square
	Berlin Wall dismantled
	Exxon Valdez spills millions of gallons of oil

1990-1999

| 1990 | Nelson Mandela released |

1990	USSR disintegrates into separate nations
	East and West Germany re-unite
	Iraqi troops invade Kuwait
	French-British Channel Tunnel bore holes meet
	Gorbachev resigns as communist rule of USSR ends
1991	Operation Desert Storm
1992	Prince Charles and Princess Diana separate
	Official end of the Cold War
1993	Cult compound in Waco, Texas raided
	World Trade Center bombed
	Internet usage begins to grow exponentially
1994	Channel tunnel opens
	Rwandan genocide
	OJ Simpson arrested for murder
1995	Oklahoma City bombing
1996	Mad Cow disease in Britain
	Unabomber arrested
1997	Mother Teresa dies
	Princess Diana dies in car crash
	Hong Kong returned to China
	Scientists clone sheep
1998	Viagra on the market
1999	Euro is European currency
1999	JFK, Jr. dies in plane crash
	Serbia attacked by NATO

2000-2009

2000	The human genome is mapped
	Concorde crashes near Paris
2001	9/11 in the USA
	Taliban regime collapses

2002	Terrorists kill hundreds in Bali
2003	The Columbia Shuttle explodes
	The Iraqi War begins
2004	Indonesian Tsunami kills thousands
	Terrorist attacks in Spain
2005	Hurricane Katrina
	London hit by terrorist bombings
2006	Saddam Hussein convicted
2007	US sends troops to Iraq
2008	Fidel Castro steps down after 49 years
	Barrack Obama elected first black president of the US
2009	Michael Jackson dies

2010-2016

2010	7.0 Earthquake hits Haiti; 200,000 dead
2011	9.0 Japan earthquake damages nuclear power plant
	Arab Spring
	Osama bin Laden killed
2012	London Olympic Games
	Hurricane Sandy
	Encyclopedia Britannica ceases its print edition
2013	Nelson Mandela dies
2014	Sochi Winter Olympics
2014	Crisis in Ukraine
2015	Massacres in Nigeria by the Boko Haram group
	Apple releases the iWatch
	Justin Trudeau elected Prime Minister of Canada
2016	Donald Trump elected President of the United States

About the Author

Marva K. Blackmore lives in Qualicum Beach on Vancouver Island, British Columbia.

A professional performing storyteller, she has told stories internationally and at venues across Canada, delighting audiences at festivals, coffee houses and on concert stages.

She is the founder and Artistic Director of Tales for the Telling, Storytelling for Adults, at the McMillan Arts Centre in Parksville, BC, which showcases professional storytellers from Canada and the United States performing juried programs. A Past President of the Storytellers of Canada, she has written and produced successful storytelling shows incorporating stories and music including: "W-interlude: Christmas Music in Story and Song" and "Turn Your Radio on: Gospel Music in Story and Song."

She teaches courses in Storytelling and also leads workshops in Memoir Writing Using Storytelling Techniques. If you are interested in having her present a workshop on Memoir Writing, she can be reached by e-mail at storyteller.marva@shaw.ca or through her websites at tellingyourstory.ca or www.wordweaver.info

Telling Your Story:

The Series

Watch for upcoming titles in the "Telling Your Story" series to accompany *Telling Your Story: A Guide to Writing Your Memoir Stories*.

Telling Your Story: The Workbook: It's All About Practice

Telling Your Story: Don't let the Grammar Gods Defeat You

Telling Your Story: Time to Rewrite: The Editing Process

Telling Your Story: Time to Publish: What are Your Options?